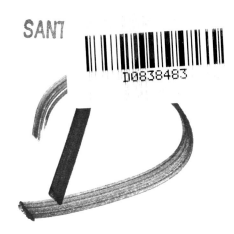

RUNNING
5K AND 10K

A TRAINING GUIDE

RUNNING
5K AND 10K

A TRAINING GUIDE

DAVID CHALFEN

THE CROWOOD PRESS

First published in 2014 by
The Crowood Press Ltd
Ramsbury, Marlborough
Wiltshire SN8 2HR

www.crowood.com

British Library Cataloguing-in-Publication Data
A catalogue record for this book is available from the British Library.

ISBN 978 1 84797 796 0

Photo Credits
Urban Bettag, Simon Parker, Run England, Rosa Chalfen

Dedication
To my mother Diane and my sister Julia

Typeset by Jean Cussons Typesetting, Diss, Norfolk

Printed and bound in India by Replika Press Pvt Ltd

CONTENTS

ABOUT THE AUTHOR

David Chalfen has been coaching endurance running for over a decade and has been running for over thirty years. He is a Level 4 Performance UKA Coach and is an Area Endurance Coach Mentor for England Athletics, developing the endurance coaching network in north London and Hertfordshire. He has coached numerous distance runners ranging from national level to modest club level, and operates both as a volunteer coach – as a member of Serpentine Running Club – and via a website *www.runcoach1to1.com.*

He has also acted as Team Manager for various international athletes at major marathons in Europe and Asia and has written feature articles about endurance running for *Athletics Weekly.* He competed at County level and ran ten marathons under 2 hours 35 minutes, with a best of 2.32. He lives in London. He was educated in north London and at Oxford University. This is his second book for Crowood. His first was *Improve Your Marathon and Half Marathon Running..*

CHAPTER 1

INTRODUCTION: BEING A RUNNER

Who is This Book For?

So who is this book pitched at, and why? Well, it's definitely not a true beginner's book as it assumes that the reader has gone through the newbie stage and has dealt with some or all of the basic issues and concerns that people may have about simply getting into a regular running routine. It also assumes that you are currently doing some structured, varied-paced running beyond simply heading out the door to build up 'time on feet' – or at least, physically and mentally you are in a state of readiness to do so. It is also intended to be of real practical use to the large numbers of new coaches, assistant coaches and leaders in running, who, having done the course and assessment, should find the book provides varied practical support as to how the theory works in reality.

The book is *not* targeted at advanced or very experienced club runners who are already hitting the roads, trails or tracks most days each week, and who have built up some structure of long runs, intervals, threshold efforts and steady runs and who have at least some understanding of why they do what they do.

The core of the training schedules in the book are structured around a pattern of four runs per week and hover around a range of 20 to 30 miles per week (or 30 to 40 kilometres). The training plans and advice detailed in

Chapter 2 are focused on the 5k and 10k race distances, but will be very relevant to most people pursuing goals from 3k/2 miles up to 10 miles and, with some reservations, even half marathon.

In some ways this book is intended as a twenty-first century revamp of the two excellent books by former *Sunday Times* athletics correspondent Cliff Temple (published in 1979 and 1981 and now sadly out of print). He coached up to what was then world-class level (and indeed his 2.28 marathon protégée Sarah Rowell is a fellow Crowood author), but had very modest running prowess himself, having just nipped under a 3-hour marathon at his best. In the 'club runner' section of his first book, the template for basic marathon competency was a sub 3-hour target. Try that today and you immediately alienate about 95 per cent of potential readers, as this author discovered with his first running blog for *The Guardian* in 2013. Interestingly, Temple used a 40-mile week as the starting point for his sub 3-hour plan, which peaked with one at 100 miles. No quick wins in the late '70s. He also included 10-mile races as staple competitive options – a nice distance which has now, sadly, become a rare event. This would be particularly handy for newer runners whose half marathon times broadly match the world's leading runners at the marathon.

One of the biggest changes since the '80s is the vast array of information about running available on the internet. In many ways this can be helpful, but, on the other hand, the sheer volume of information, much of it provided by people with modest credentials and a clear commercial bias which stresses that their product or service is the key to running progress, means that many relative newcomers to the sport can become confused about what will make the biggest difference to their running. Beetroot juice or a physiological test? Minimalist shoes or compression socks? A long, slow fat-burning run or a lung-bursting interval session? With so many runners leading increasingly busy lives, people just don't have the time or inclination to sift through the reams of web-based content that may or may not be relevant.

Another advance that maybe clouds the picture for the 'mid pack' runner is the ever-increasing amount of scientific research that seems to have potential relevance to how they train. At one extreme, there is the cutting-edge élite work carried out as part of many countries' investment in high performance sport, and the UK is one of the world leaders in this field. At the other extreme is the vast amount of research on basic cardio-vascular fitness and health. This can be confusing for the average runner. How relevant or replicable is something that will shave a few tenths of a second off Mo Farah's final lap in a 5,000m race? And what is the cost vs benefit for them, given it's not likely to be the same as it is for Mo? At the other extreme, for regular runners trying to dip under 22 minutes in their local 5k park run, how much use to their training is something that shows 'get fit quick' benefits to obese people leading highly sedentary lives?

As one example, I recently saw a TV item about a Japanese scientist, who had devised a training protocol that was seen as the absolute optimum way of getting the most intense and quickest aerobic benefits in the shortest time possible, in terms of the length of the sessions and their frequency. The training was done on a spin bike. Of course, if you are a very busy person trying to improve your running and someone suggests you can achieve in 45 minutes per week what you are currently spending maybe 4 hours per week doing, you'll be interested. This particular training method was, in essence, eight efforts of 30 seconds at your *absolute maximum* with a fairly short and only partial recovery in between. I'd be surprised if more than 1 per cent of readers of this book currently do any training of this nature – partly because it is intensely uncomfortable and few runners would actually be able to complete the full session; and partly because the session is very highly anaerobic, and for a 5k/10k training plan that critical level of intensity doesn't need to be practised very often. What was slightly galling from the perspective of an endurance running coach was that the training session was seen as something new, when in fact, in terms of the structure of the session and the challenge to the aerobic and anaerobic energy systems, it would be something that every 400/800m runner, every 100m swimmer, every 1k bike time trialist and every 500m canoe sprinter would be broadly familiar with.

State of the (Running) Nation

We've all heard the simple mantra that 'running is the cheapest sport; all you need is a T-shirt, a pair of shorts and a pair of trainers'. Well, that's true up to a point, and there are indeed some young African runners who get by on not much more than this basic kit bag. However, the economics of running for the vast majority have now gone way beyond this subsistence model. Indeed, there are races (if 'races' is the right word, maybe 'experience' is more apt) where the entry fee can hit four

Women are the majority in most new running groups.

figures, and that's before you actually travel to the event. We aren't talking here about a warm-up jog to the local park.

Even in the three years or so since I was commissioned to write my first book, the world of running, in the UK at least, has noticeably changed. Maybe it's overstating it, but more than ever before I sometimes feel that there are two separate sports: competitive running, where people see themselves as part of a system that leads to international level, albeit for many they are just part of the system rather than likely to actually put on a national team vest; and an ever-increasing majority, for whom running isn't a sport in the traditional competitive sense where people did it to see how good they could become at it, but more of a low-key recreational activity.

Even the usual overarching position, whereby the national governing body for a sport has some sort of stake in every participant from élite to novice, has become very questionable in distance running. If UK Athletics didn't exist then by and large Mo Farah has enough knowledge, support networks and money to buy whatever it takes to keep him at the cutting edge of the sport. At the other end, there are thousands of low level recreational runners who can simply do their own thing, training solo or in informal groups, entering park runs for free or commercially organized road races for a higher entry fee, with minimal direct benefit from a governing body.

The England Athletics document mentioned below presents a county-based snapshot of this diversity. Using the sparsely populated county of Wiltshire, it shows almost fifty running groups. The traditional stalwarts such as Swindon Harriers and City of Salisbury Athletics and Running Club barely get a look in amidst the posses of Trotters, Sisters, Beginners, Violets, All Stars and Hounds, though, thankfully, Runners still seems to be the most frequently used collective noun for the activity they all offer.

It's hard to articulate this without being misinterpreted as élitist or old-fashioned; and it's all tied up with a load of social, cultural and even political contexts. To illustrate the latter, a couple of anecdotes. 'Regular participation' is now measured as 1×30 minutes a week. Many 'retention' programmes count eight sessions as 'retained'. When one spends a good proportion of coaching time dealing with people running 50 miles a week (say, 7 hours) as their norm, and a few others running close to double this, it's sometimes hard to really empathize with this sort of approach. It's also true that the novelty event profile has moved on in some ways. In an environment where PBs seem less of a pursuit for many, and it becomes more about the buzz, it's not obvious to the author why – to quote two examples – having the start and finish of an event marked by a London Routemaster bus is a particular cachet, or why doing a 5k (which actually wasn't even 5k) while receiving a load of multicoloured paint thrown over your kit en route is an enticing attraction. However, let's be clear on this: as separate options both buses and paint have their own merits and society would be a poorer place without them. If you've actually bought this book, though, I presume you are perched on the performance side of the recreational running perspective.

Group warm-ups can be part of running's social side.

At the time of finalizing this manuscript England Athletics produced *A Nation That Runs*, probably the first publication of this kind focused specifically on defining and quantifying the 'market' segments for the sport. It found that 5.95 million people in England have run at least once in the last twelve months, so they are the current running population. It is, to say the least, a rather loose frequency of participation and, for the purposes of this book, in those 364 non-running days they are perhaps letting their 5k/10k potential drift a tad. One in three runners has what is officially a 'frequent running habit' – that is, at least one bout of 30 minutes per week – and about 8 per cent (475,000) people run in organized running events.

Running and Shopping

There is an ever-growing array of technological equipment and event options that even twenty-five years ago, when the recreational running market was fairly substantial, didn't exist. And of course the crusty old purist in me can't help but mention that as the array of 'runner as consumer' products and services grows ever more diverse and numerous, not to mention costly, so the average performance of everyone involved in actually doing the running is on a gradual downward trend. I'm definitely not claiming a cause and effect link – it's more complex than that – but the words 'woods' and 'trees' come to mind.

Having coached many scores of runners across a very wide range of performance levels, I have noticed a strong trend that the highest performers and hardest trainers tend to go fairly light on buying into the full array of technology. They have the simplest, most old-fashioned training diaries – indeed several actually have pens and paper on the go for

this purpose. While they check out products that may make a very small but worthwhile gain in performance without them necessarily having to train further or harder, they distinguish these from a 'short cut' or 'quick win' mentality. From experience, and speaking generally, I would suggest that, shoes and kit aside, you should prioritise something for sports medicine at the forefront of your running budget. Whether it be medical insurance and/or regular physiotherapy/massage/osteopath treatment, the icing on the cake options for fine-tuning are not much help when the cake is a set of fractured crumbs.

For the large majority of people reading this book, the high performance aspect won't be their particular passion, but hopefully there will be a few who have that combination of commitment, curiosity to test their limits, capacity to train hard for some years and maybe some good genetic luck to make bigger waves with their running.

Running Groups

With the growth of running at most levels, and because national governing bodies seeking ongoing government funding need to show that their work is having a direct impact on raising participation, England Athletics has developed its officially branded programme which has been very successful in helping grow the scale of recreational running. Its Regional Coordinator in the West of England is Charlotte Fisher, who says:

'For the absolute beginner, putting one's trainers on and heading out of the front door for a run can be a daunting personal challenge. Will I get to the end of the road without getting out of breath? What if someone sees me out running? What if I look silly? What if I need the loo? What do I do with my arms?

New running groups are emerging in big numbers.

What if I have to stop and walk? – are just some of the many questions beginner runners ask.'

Fisher continues: 'The traditional club environment can unintentionally be an intimidating place for a beginner to start their running journey. The vision of packs of club runners in very short shorts and vests or Lycra-clad kit whizzing along the pavements at anything from 8-minute miles to 5-minute miles is an intimidating one. "Run England" (www.runengland.org) is the recreational running programme from England Athletics and provides a great starting point for beginners, as well as improvers, through a supportive group environment. Groups vary from small friendly groups of eight or so runners to much larger groups with several sub-groups for walk/run, beginner and improver sessions. There are over 2,000 registered Run England groups

Run England at work and play.

to choose from and they all come with a UK Athletics licensed leader. The leaders are trained to understand the barriers that stop people running and to provide appropriate sessions for beginners. There are groups all across the country to meet the needs of the beginner runner, with weekday and weekend, evening and daytime sessions, meeting in parks, community centres and workplaces.'

Fisher is herself an interesting reflection of the current diversity and evolution of the sport. In a voluntary capacity at the 'traditional' athletics club in Taunton she coaches an increasingly successful squad of national level middle-distance runners in the Under-17 to Under-23 groups, while earning her living in the less performance-focused end of the sport.

The worries that new runners have can remind established runners and coaches that some of the things that we treat almost as instinct do have to be learned at some stage. This brings to mind an anecdote from Olympic Marathon medallist Charlie Spedding, who was asked by a newcomer at a training forum for his views on breathing. 'Highly recommended,' he replied.

There are numerous individual and group case histories which show just how motivational the group environment can be for those coming to the sport without any background in it, and often without any sporting experience beyond school PE lessons. Run leader Angie Tiller from Falmouth, Cornwall, says: 'Some of the trainees admitted that the warm-up was in itself the most exercise they'd done in years… I've been astounded by what people are capable of achieving in a group setting in a relatively short period of time.'

Moving into the gritty urban environment of inner London we find a slightly different variation on the running group theme. Notably, Run Dem Crew, whose name sounds like they should be knocking out heavy bass lines in a darkened nightclub, but who are in fact an organized and fast-growing running group with, at the time of writing, a main base in Clerkenwell, just north of the City of London, and a west London section near Paddington Station. The particular traits of this group are that the runners are predominantly young – on the night the author ran with them he was by some margin the oldest runner, and about 95 per cent of the group of about 40 were younger than 35 years old. They were split about 50/50 by gender, and the ethnic

Run Dem Crew are a fast-growing group of young adult runners in London.

diversity was much closer to the London demography than most running groups have yet managed to achieve.

Despite perhaps being unaware of the history of the sport, they have in effect become a 'third wave' running group, following first the athletic and harrier clubs and second what we should probably no longer call the 'new breed' of running clubs that sprang up in the wake of the first London Marathon in the early 1980s. That said, the RDC seen 'at the coal face' do not seem that radically different from many urban or suburban running clubs. They run regularly, they have training sessions with some structure and intensity to them, they do races, they have a social element, they are genuinely welcoming to people who want to take part and improve, they have some qualified run leaders and new coaches, and they too are affiliated to England Athletics. It was interesting that in such an informal social setting virtually every runner doing the group session worked very hard at it, suggesting that in essence nearly everyone who tries any kind of structured running has some sort of performance and improvement ethos motivating them.

Goal-Setting

This will sound a bit like fence-sitting, but until you have some sort of history of short-term running progression and/or some sort

Regrouping between some urban interval efforts.

of transferred aerobic base from another endurance sport, the precision of goal-setting against the clock is just number-crunching, and usually round numbers. Overstating the theme somewhat, it seems that every 10k runner between 40.30 and 44.59 has sub-40 as the next goal. At the slower end of the spectrum, that's a 12 per cent increase. For many that will be achievable, and in some cases there will be plenty more scope for progression, but do look at things in context.

The big gains invariably come in the earliest months of training, often combined with some level of weight loss and some moves towards a healthier lifestyle. You can only give up the daily fry-ups, late nights and tequila slammers once, just as you can only go from being a non-runner to a regular runner once. The closest you might get to repeating the 'new runner' scenario would be if you had to have significant time off training due to illness or injury, and the early stages of the comeback would see you making improvements rapidly.

At the top end of the spectrum, where the diminishing returns principle applies most acutely, the UK Athletics élite performance programme looks broadly for a 1 per cent annual increase from its senior world-class athletes, and about 2 per cent per annum in the junior élite development squad. That's one hell of a lot of training, sacrifice, and medical and conditioning back-up to go not very much faster. Do the maths – for a 50-minute 10k runner that's 1 minute over a year.

Be aware, therefore, that if you follow a few cycles of the training programmes in this volume, you may eventually reach a plateau. The schedules do, however, provide notes on how you can push the boat out a little more to make further progress.

Be mindful that, physiologically, you will reach your VO_2 max (described in Chapter 2) after a relatively short time if you train appropriately. Some while later you will lack the scope to improve your lactate turnpoint/anaerobic threshold, and typically the last key parameter to start levelling off is your running economy. We are talking years here rather than months, but it does lead one to the slightly stodgy message that you need to be patient, stick with the running for years and, as your experience and mileage history build up,

The sharp end at Alexandra Palace.

Most road relays have stages between 4k and 10k.

accept that it is the simple repetition of getting out the door and running steady miles that becomes a key part of longer term improvement. Quick wins are quick, and they are limited.

Linked to this is the typical pattern that if, as many do, you are racing over a range of long distances relatively early in your running days, for example from 5k park runs to marathons, your performances over these distances will progress broadly in line with the relative significance of VO_2 max, lactate threshold and running economy respectively.

This won't be something that you can measure empirically, but in my experience newer runners can underestimate the effect on race performance that the combination of hot weather, hills and particularly off-road surfaces can have. The plus side of this is that if you have raced mainly in warm weather, or on hilly courses where plenty of the underfoot surface is not tarmac, you may not yet have earned a PB that really reflects what you can do. Conversely, once you have done a race where everything in the environment is just right, and you have paced it optimally for your fitness at that stage, you may need to await a similarly ideal scenario before you can next trim your PB. It may be necessary for you to do a few tougher races where your relative performance is slightly better but the watch indicates otherwise. Having gone through the physical and physiological aspects that should inform your goal-setting, also factor in how mental skills can be relevant to what you will achieve, long and short term, and ponder on how the contents of Chapter 11 may apply.

Run England has a network of 1-, 2- and 3-mile routes.

A RUNNING LIFESTYLE

A fairly well-known journalist on a national newspaper gained a place on the London Marathon in April. In an article on his build-up in the February before the event he described how the training plan he had been given was now hitting 20 miles per week, and he then launched into a moan about how unreasonable it was that his entire social, family and even professional life should be put on hold while he tried to restructure things to fit in this outrageously demanding commitment.

Seeing as there are many runners who can knock out 20-mile runs at the weekend and still be back for elevenses, I thought this a rather exaggerated case of journalistic licence. It did, however, flag up that if you approach a running goal as a real outsider to the sport, the numerous subtle 'evolutionary' changes that most regular runners, of whatever level of performance, gradually make may seem somewhat disruptive and radical. The most obvious changes to many may be around food, hydration and alcohol, but the little lifestyle adjustments can broaden out to include when and where you go on holiday; what you wear on your feet during the day; what time you go to bed; how you arrange childcare; how you structure your working day and travel to and from work; how often you shower.

There's also, for more serious runners, and particularly those in the depths of marathon training, the residual fatigue that can become almost one's default feeling, so that even if you have time for certain leisure activities that were part of your pre-running life, you may just lack the energy to go for them.

Four runs a week of maybe 25 to 30 miles total, which is where most of the training detail in this book is pitched, is in some ways not a massive commitment in terms of time or energy. But, if it is added to an already full and busy life, it can leave the runner on the borderline of fatigue and under-recovery.

CHAPTER 2

GENERAL PRINCIPLES OF TRAINING

In this section, which many seasoned runners will be at least partly familiar with, we look briefly at how endurance running is fuelled, at the key systemic changes we need to improve to aid long-distance performance, and we introduce the overarching training structures to achieve these improvements. This sets the context for the more detailed training advice and schedules in subsequent chapters.

How It Works

In brief, the main energy form used in human muscle is adenosine triphosphate (ATP), a high-energy compound whose breakdown converts its chemical energy into mechanical energy, or muscle contraction. ATP is essential for the muscle to contract, but muscle stores of ATP are very limited, enough for a second or two at the most. For the muscle to continue to contract, ATP must be replenished. The speed at which you can continue to run depends on your ability to replenish ATP in your active muscles.

Sports scientists have classified three distinct human muscle energy pathways, ranked in order of their ability to replenish ATP.

1. The adenosine triphosphate-phospho-creatine (ATP-PCr) energy pathway is designed to replace ATP very rapidly.

Phosphocreatine (PCr) releases energy to synthesize ATP very rapidly but, like ATP, PCr content in the muscle is also limited. The ATP-PCr energy pathway is predominant in very short-duration, high-power events and lasts about 8 seconds. It is therefore of almost negligible significance in fuelling long-distance running performance.

2. The lactic acid energy pathway, more technically known as anaerobic glycolysis, involves the rapid breakdown of muscle glycogen (glycolysis) under conditions when oxygen supply is limited (anaerobic). It replenishes ATP less rapidly but in greater quantities than the ATP-PCr energy pathway and is the predominant energy pathway in more prolonged sprints, such as 400m. Accumulation of lactate (lactic acid) in the blood induces muscle fatigue, so the endurance of this energy pathway is somewhat limited. However, lactate itself is a powerful energy source and the painful effect caused by its accumulation is because it is stored with an attached hydrogen ion. This ion is acidic, changes the ph level of the blood from its more alkali nature and restricts the pathway of oxygen, thus leading to a rapidly increasing level of fatigue. Broadly speaking, you can run in a predominantly anaerobic state for about 60 to 70 seconds, which is obviously crucial in 800m and 1500m

races, but it becomes an ever-decreasing part of performance as the race distance increases.

3. The oxygen energy pathway involves the aerobic metabolism of either carbohydrate (aerobic glycolysis) or fat (aerobic lipolysis), producing substantial quantities of ATP but at a slower rate than the other two pathways. The oxygen energy pathway predominates in longer aerobic endurance events. Although both carbohydrate and fat may be used as fuel sources for the oxygen energy pathway, carbohydrate is the more efficient fuel. Carbohydrate produces more ATP per unit of oxygen than does fat.

Long-distance running depends primarily on the oxygen energy pathway. Its optimal functioning during long-distance events is dependent on various body systems.

For example, the digestive system is essential to provide fuel for muscular energy before and during performance. The endocrine system secretes hormones such as insulin and epinephrine that influence fuel supply to the muscle. The integumentary system, which includes the skin, is involved in temperature regulation, particularly important under warm environmental conditions.

However, the two key system combinations involved in the aerobic pathway are the neuromuscular and cardiovascular-respiratory systems. The neuromuscular system (nervous and muscle systems), which consists of the brain, peripheral nerves and muscles, generates the muscular energy to run with the appropriate speed and efficiency. The cardiovascular and respiratory systems, which consist of the heart, blood vessels and lungs, provide oxygen, the keystone to the aerobic pathway.

The interaction of the neuromuscular and cardiovascular-respiratory energy systems determines several of the key components of running potential:

- **Maximal oxygen uptake (VO_2 max)** measures the ability of the cardiovascular system to deliver and the neuromuscular system to utilize oxygen during running. It is of course related to bodyweight so is expressed per kilogram of bodyweight. You can probably run at your velocity at VO_2 max (vVO_2 max) for about 6 minutes, so it is about your 1-mile race pace.
- The **lactate threshold** or **turnpoint** (often referred to as the anaerobic threshold, perhaps less precisely because even at lower levels of effort there is an element of anaerobic energy being produced) represents the level of running intensity at which energy production becomes increasingly anaerobic, leading to lactate accumulation in the blood and increased fatigue.
- **Running economy** refers to the ability of the neuromuscular and cardiovascular-respiratory systems to maximize oxygen efficiency, obtaining the highest running speed for the amount of oxygen used. Speed represents the ability of the neuromuscular system to maximize energy production for running.

In general, improvement in any of these components will enhance your endurance running performance. 5ks will be run at slightly quicker than your speed at lactate turnpoint. 10ks will be at a speed that is very close to your turnpoint – which side of the line you fall on will be largely a result of how quickly you can race a 10k. Marathons and half marathons are run at a pace just below the lactate threshold. At every race distance, improving your running economy, which is an increase in speed at a given oxygen uptake, is a key element.

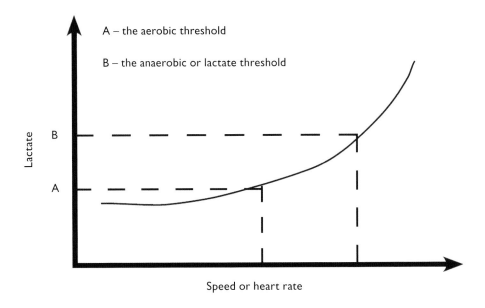

A – the aerobic threshold

B – the anaerobic or lactate threshold

Graph showing the lactate threshold/turnpoint.

What We Want From It

So you need to improve your ability in the above three parameters to progress your long-distance running performance. The training you do will:

- improve the cardiovascular system to transport blood and oxygen. Increases in heart pumping capacity, total blood volume, and capillarization of muscle tissues are some principal changes induced through suitable training;
- improve the ability of the muscles to effectively use oxygen by converting carbohydrate and fat into ATP. Increases in the size and number of mitochondria, oxidative enzymes, and myoglobin in oxidative muscle fibres are beneficial changes.

Collectively, these adaptations to training will:

- improve aerobic capacity (VO_2 max)
- improve the lactate threshold, so it is attained at a faster running speed
- improve running economy by lowering the energy demand of running
- improve speed, or the ability of the neuromuscular system to maximize energy production for running.

How We Improve It

Before we look at how to build up the training specifics, it is helpful to ensure we understand the principles of why we train at all.

The usual rationale for the benefits of training is about adaptation and super-compensation. This applies to any sports training. Put simply, you challenge the body's limit of a particular performance factor, which then fatigues the body, giving it a short-term dip. It then gradually recovers, restores itself to the original level and then – the 'super-compensation effect' – adds a small margin of additional capacity at whatever element it has been challenged at. It's also notable that different types of running session will have a beneficial effect on more than one parameter of endurance performance.

Because regular training means training on most days, it is very hard to put a timeline on how long this process takes in full, because any hard training session will always have various other training stimuli on preceding and succeeding days, each with their own benefits. However, most experienced athletes and coaches think that it takes about 10 to 12 days to get the full benefit of a training session. It follows, therefore, that when looking at a target race and planning a taper, particularly for longer races, you should go back about 12 days beforehand to your last key, race-specific training session. After this, the training focus should be on maintenance and avoiding detraining. If you look at how an élite athlete trained for a big race you will often see a big, hard, specific session 10 to 12 days before.

Rates of Improvement – the Genetic Lottery

It's worth mentioning that a major factor in a runner's rate of improvement will be the make-up of their slow twitch and fast twitch fibres. Put simply, we have three types of muscle fibres:

- Type 1 – slow twitch (red), best suited to aerobic energy production
- Type 2a – fast twitch oxidative (white), which can also be trained to take on the aerobic efficiency of Type 1 fibres but if not trained aerobically are in essence used

for more speed-based energy requirements
- Type 2b – fast twitch glycolytic, which use the anaerobic (glycolytic) energy system and cannot be adapted to operate aerobically.

The large majority of untrained people have a fast twitch vs slow twitch balance that falls between 45 per cent to 55 per cent of each type. The world élite are genetic outliers who have around 80 per cent slow twitch (long distance) or 80 per cent fast twitch (sprinters). The same trends would be apparent in other sports, depending on where the sport fits in the spectrum between speed and endurance.

It is not known exactly how the adaptation of Type 2a to Type 1 fibres occurs, nor is there any data that draws clear links between what a few extra per cent of slow twitch fibres is 'worth' in performance terms. On a practical level there is nothing you can do to change your composition of Type 2b fibres. What you may notice is that, if you are training with others, a key factor in how quickly people improve their endurance performance, and indeed the level at which they level off when they are training at close to their maximum capacity, is how well-endowed they are with slow twitch fibres.

The Events' Physiological Basis

It's useful to be aware of the energy requirements of the various endurance events. Some readers may be surprised to learn that the governing body of the sport (International Association of Athletics Federations – IAAF) officially treats 'endurance running' as all events from 800m upwards, and national governing bodies follow suit. This impacts upon national and regional club structures, coaching, competitions and, filtering down to

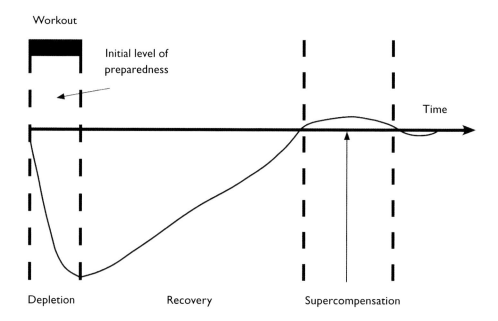

Workout

Initial level of preparedness

Time

Depletion   Recovery   Supercompensation

Super-compensation graph.

an individual level, it means a significant amount of common ground shared by 800m runners and marathoners, even though the latter is some fifty-two times the race distance. The main common feature, which the table below illustrates, is that the main energy source is aerobic; this is why the endurance event group is defined as it is.

It should be noted that these figures will vary slightly depending on what test protocol is used, and also that those shown below are based on high performance runners. The slower the runner is over a given race distance, the higher the aerobic percentage will become, because with the anaerobic element only able to be sustained for a very short time, the longer the race duration, the less proportion can be spent in an anaerobic state. So the aerobic/anaerobic energy split of a 50-minute 10k runner will be more in line with an élite half marathoner than an élite 10k runner. Perhaps the main training element where mid-pack long-distance runners go astray from the event's requirements is either in doing too much anaerobic training or in putting too much store in how they perform in the occasional anaerobic training that they do. Remember, your lactate tolerance at above your anaerobic threshold level will only show in the final 60 to 90 seconds of performance; the further up the race distances you go, the less significance it will have. So, showboating down the final 100m of the final rep in a 400m interval session won't help you sustain target pace in the ninth kilometre of a 10k race.

Event	Aerobic Energy per cent	Anaerobic Energy per cent	ATP per cent
800m	40	51	9
1500m	67	28	5
3,000m	82	16	2
5,000m	90	9	1
10,000m	95	4	<1
Half Marathon	98	2	<1
Marathon	99+	<1	<1

Which Training Paces for Which Benefits?

The table overleaf shows the relative benefits of respective training paces, going from the easiest recovery pace to the most full-on speedwork, and giving a relative weighting for each pace against each criterion you are trying to improve. The overall takeaway message should be that even when you have a particular focus for a particular run, there will be more than one performance box that you are ticking. There is clearly a mixture of art and science in putting together the optimum combination of these factors – and it's the 'art' bit which means you won't find any perfect set of numbers that will tell you exactly how to structure every part of every training run or session.

Another factor to bear in mind is that these physiological zones are often presented in an élite athlete context, so, for example, velocity at VO_2 max (or vVO_2 max) is often simplistically described as '3k race pace'. That's fine if you are Mo Farah, clicking off seven laps of the track at 60 seconds each, but for many runners their vVO_2 max will be far closer to their 1-mile/1500m race pace. Even for a 38- to 40-minute 10k runner it will correspond more closely to their notional 2k race pace. And so it is with the sort of physiological parameters allocated to élite runners' 10k and marathon race paces.

The training schedules in these chapters mix and balance these factors to match the level of 5k and 10k runners.

Adding Some Structure to Improvement

This is where we now start crossing over from the scientist's domain into the coach's territory.

The flip side of the preceding point about training adaptations is that they are reversible. In simple terms, 'use it or lose it!' So, for example, if you do a hard session at your target 10k pace on Day 1 of a cycle, then sometime around Days 10 to 12 you will reap the benefit if you test yourself. But if you then neglect to challenge yourself again at that sort of intensity, the benefit from the effort made on Day 1 will start to gradually seep away. In the short term the amounts, if we expressed them either as a percentage or in seconds per mile or per kilometre, are small, and particularly so if we isolate them to just one

GENERAL PRINCIPLES OF TRAINING

	Recovery/ easy	Steady/ comfortable – slightly slower than marathon pace	Steady/less comfortable – quicker than marathon pace	10-mile to half marathon pace	10k to 10 mile pace	vVO2 max – 2k to 3 k race pace	Faster than 1500m race pace
Increased blood volume	*	****	****	***	*		
Stimulates aerobic enzymes		***	***	***	****	*	
Stimulates fatty acids as fuel source	*	****	***	**	*		
Improved use of lactate as a fuel				**	***	***	****
Increased maximum rate of muscle glycogen usage				**	****	****	***
Increased capillarization	*	***	****	***	***	**	*
Improved blood and muscle buffering capacity				**	***	****	****
Increased maximum cardiac output			*	**	***	***	****
Increased ventilatory capacity				*	***	****	****
Improved neuro muscular adaption		*	*	***	****	***	***

**** Maximum effect *** Very strong effect ** Significant effect * Limited effect

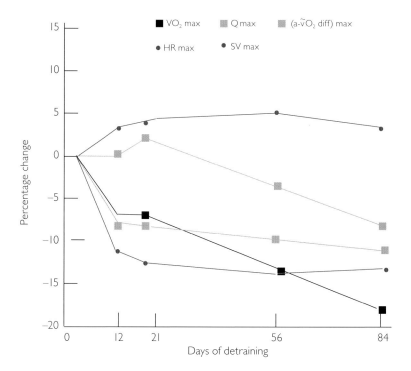

Effect of detraining on VO$_2$ max.

training session, but over a few months the loss of event-specific fitness would be more striking.

On a practical planning basis one can see a link between the approximate time to absorb the benefit of a session, and the 14-day training cycle around which many plans are structured. Broadly, this gives the athlete one session per cycle at each of the four or five main levels of intensity around which they are building their training.

Another cornerstone of training principles, particularly for more seasoned runners, is that once the body has gone through a repeated cycle of a particular training stimulus, the response to that stimulus will, in the short term, probably have been maximized, so there is greater benefit in doing something different and drawing the benefit from a new stimulus. We are considering this all within the context of what is of performance benefit to endurance running, so when talking of variety we don't mean sideline the threshold running and play 9 holes of golf instead.

A simple and relevant example could be that if you have spent eight weeks building up your long run from, say, 50 to 80 minutes all at a similar steady pace, you could then follow that with a similar period where the focus is about doing comparable distances at greater speed.

Of course, if you repeat the same long run week in week out there may still be considerable benefit and indeed you may do some pace variations within it on a 'how you feel on the day' basis, but the rate of progress is likely

Six-month Macrocycle– the full season

Mesocycle 1 – transition	Mesocycle 2 – general endurance 1	Mesocycle 3 – general endurance 2	Mesocycle 4 – specific endurance 1	Mesocycle 5 – specific endurance 2	Mesocycle 6 – peaking and competing

Each microcycle comprises a 14-day block of training and recovery

Microcycle 1 – recovery	Microcycle 3 – steady running/ threshold	Microcycle 5 – steady running/ threshold/ vVO_2 max/hills	Microcycle 7 – steady running/long distance marathon pace/hills	Microcycle 9 – steady steady running/ long distance marathon pace/ 5k/10k pace	Microcycle peaking for event steady running/ threshold/ marathon pace/ vVO_2
Microcycle 2 – transition	Microcycle 4 – steady running/ threshold/ vVO_2 max	Microcycle 6 – steady running/ threshold/ vVO_2 max/hills	Microcycle 8 – steady running/long distance/ marathon pace/ 5k/10k pace	Microcycle 10 – steady running/ threshold/ marathon pace/ 5k/10k pace	Microcycle 12 – taper/ competition

to be slower than if you are more systematic in following good practice.

My own experience is that for many seasoned and committed runners who are sensibly 'ticking the boxes' of the main physiological factors in long-distance running, the single most useful coaching benefit to add to their programme is a purposeful use of periodization. Put simply, this involves seeking to optimize the balance of each training stimulus so that nothing is left undercooked nor is anything pursued past the point at which it continues to add value. There most definitely isn't a formula for this that works for all runners all of the time. Whoever finds that formula can be the proud author of what would be the last endurance coaching book ever needing to be written.

Within these cycles, periodic recovery and 'absorption' weeks should be planned.

Most runners will find that once every three or four weeks they will benefit from reducing the training load by about one-third from the previous month's peak. This will apply to both volume and intensity. So, for example, if your weekly mileage has been 35 on average, just about 25 should be planned. You should similarly cap the harder training sessions, whatever their composition, at about two-thirds of what would be a full, challenging session. This usually gives the right balance between maintaining fitness while avoiding the risk of overtraining and preventing any 'detraining'. This downsizing should also be reflected in your strength and conditioning session(s) in the relevant week.

Of course, any number of factors such as work, domestics, even shifting around on what days you do your long run, may prevent this reduced week being an exact arithmetical two-thirds. Don't agonize over the numbers but do try to ensure that the week feels like a noticeable 'freshen up' phase. It's fairly common and logical practice to try to match these easier weeks with those that end with a race you wish to do well in.

We should emphasize at this point that amidst all the training intensities and session options, interval training produces no magic wand effect for experienced or improving runners. However, it is undoubtedly true that if all your running is at what you find either a slow or a steady comfortable pace, interval training – running faster repetitions at something close to 100 per cent of your VO2 max with a managed recovery between each fast effort – will definitely bring performance improvements more quickly and more substantially than doing the same steady state stuff day in day out.

All distance runners should make use of this training – although not all will enjoy it.

Coaching Support

By reading this book you are clearly taking an additional step in your coaching set-up. A good coach should nearly always be able to add something to an athlete's performance. The level of input and the measurement of the benefit will vary in each individual case.

If you think about the value of coaching support in the long term, its merits become maybe more demonstrable. Let's suggest that a good coach can be 'worth' an average of 2 per cent per year to an athlete's results. Typically the benefit would be greater at the outset and would reduce as the athlete becomes more experienced, knowledgeable and starts to get closer to his or her physical limit. This hypothetical 2 per cent is the 'added value' that comes on top of what the athlete may be doing off his or her own ideas on issues such as increasing mileage, structured sessions, and strength and conditioning. If you do the maths on a four-year cycle, that 4 per cent at 7 minutes per mile race pace gives about 17 seconds per mile, so maybe 1 minute

over 5k, and 2 minutes for a 10k. Maybe food for thought if you are a self-coached runner who has reached a plateau.

If you are relatively new to the sport, have not yet found a suitably holistic and individualized package of coaching wisdom on websites or in magazines, and are doing all your planning isolated from a running club structure, coaching benefits may be greater for you.

In addition to the more obvious staples of a training plan and technical knowledge, there are more subtle benefits that a coach may bring. These include:

- Motivation – not in the obvious sense of an in-your-face Mr/Ms Motivator, but the runner's awareness that the coach has spent a fair amount of time putting together a training plan, so you should feel a level of obligation to follow it if you are fit and able to do so.
- Quality assured recommendations to, for example, massagers, physiotherapists or osteopaths, podiatrists. Sometimes it seems that everybody in the medical services sector claims extensive expertise in 'sports injuries', but the number with good credentials on the specifics of endurance running is somewhat smaller and a coach can help steer you in the right direction.
- Links to training partners or groups, particularly for long runs and harder sessions where the presence of others is invariably worth a few seconds per mile compared to doing it all solo, where your mind has nothing to focus on apart from the increasing fatigue.
- Also, simply a 'third eye'. We've all had the experience of writing something like a CV or report where we've double, triple and quadruple checked it for accuracy and are convinced it is spot-on, and then when a fresh pair of eyes reads it they pick up

some typos or spelling errors. Sometimes we tell ourselves what we want to be told and our mind plays little tricks on us. A similar scenario can occur in running training, where a runner draws up a plan and has a blind spot.

If you are able to gain the advice of a coach, keep in mind the following guidelines:

- Give the coach at least three months and ideally six months to 'make a difference' unless you have a major and profound disagreement with the approach early on. Any competent coach wishing to reduce your risk of injury will evolve your training gradually, however enthusiastic you may be to revolutionize your approach overnight, and there is also a time lag needed to do the training, adapt to the benefits and perform faster.
- Seek a suitable match between your level of commitment and ambition, and the coach's, otherwise one or both of you may soon become frustrated.
- Agree with the coach what sort of parameters of frequency of communication are likely to work best, and what level of detail is needed to help inform the progression of your training. The minutiae of whether you had a third piece of toast for breakfast or whether your threshold run lost 57 seconds because of red traffic lights delaying you can probably be kept to yourself, but a weekly or fortnightly update is usually helpful for both parties.
- In an increasingly contract-based society, voluntary sports coaching has very few mutual obligations as long as the coach acts within what the relevant coaching licence's code of conduct requires. The world of sports coaching is certainly changing its shift between voluntary and paid coaches. There are no absolute rights and wrongs on what model works best but the principles of good coaching, across the technical, communication and behavioural aspects, should be followed as well as possible whether the coach is working for a fee or as a volunteer.

CHAPTER 3

THE TRAINING PLANS

Let's try to be creative with the labelling of categories here: no beginners, intermediate and advanced. Why not? Because a genuine beginner will for some weeks be simply building up the slow running/jogging pace interspersed with walking recoveries, with the walk recovery time and frequency gradually reducing. And that's barely a training schedule, more a basic aerobic fitness plan, although one wouldn't want to defend the difference between the two under cross-examination by a QC. Nor on the other hand are we looking at genuinely advanced runners who are probably training at a level of pace, volume and frequency just beyond where this book is pitched, and who, one hopes, have largely already gathered the knowledge that is offered here. So if we have just 'intermediate' we need to split that category somehow. We'll wrestle with the available vocabulary and go for schedules aimed at Improvement and then Progression – in effect, two stages to fill the gap between beginner and advanced.

Where do you fit in? That's the tricky bit. Ponder on this. Rachel is 25 years old and a new runner, in that she has never had any involvement in structured running and hasn't even done informal regular running since she was 13 years old at school. She doesn't really know about running training. But here's the thing. As a 12-year-old Rachel reluctantly won her school's inter-house cross-country race – not because she was that fussed about it, but because it was quite uncomfortable running

2 kilometres at full effort, so she thought she would get it done and dusted as fast as she could and be in time to get to her drama lesson, her favourite. But Rachel was a good and keen swimmer and trained up to six times a week with the main City club until she was 14, when it all became a drain on her life. Then at university she got into rowing, doing the lightweights because at 5ft 6in and 9 stone she was much too small to be in the full squad. She trained five days a week and got slightly drunk on the other two days. So Rachel is a new runner but she's clearly an aerobic beast (a technical but unscientific term; coaches know what it means and can, very excitedly, spot one at fifty paces), who historically knows what hard endurance training is about, both the 'feel' of it and, subconsciously maybe, how the different training efforts are structured. She won't be spending very long at all on the jog/walk scenario.

Conversely, let's look at Jim. He's 47 and has been running regularly for three years. He never did any sport at school beyond basic PE and as he had little natural speed, endurance or hand-eye coordination he received little support from PE teachers. At age 40 he was smoking twenty-five a day, drinking about twenty-five pints of beer each week, except around Christmas and holidays and birthdays when it was topped up with wine, and eating takeaways about three nights a week when the combination of very long days travelling with his work and having little time with his family meant that he frequently didn't get

Try to vary the running surface.

to eat balanced meals. He was pushing 15 stone/95 kilos, at a height of 5ft 10in. But then Jim decided to start jogging, worried about the effect that this unhealthy lifestyle was having on his basic health, so that walking up the escalator at Euston Station left him out of breath and sweaty. He gave up the cigs, cut the alcohol by more than half, and reined in the takeaways. He had some months doing that jog/walk programme so that after twelve weeks he could jog 4 miles continuously in just over 40 minutes. But Jim is a normal guy with no great endurance talent or ambition, and his job is still as demanding as ever, his kids still need his support and attention and his meals, if not the nightmare stuff of old, are still fairly high in saturated fat, salt and added sugar. But by and large Jim goes running three times a week, or sometimes two. He does between 30 and 40 minutes each time. He still weighs about 13 and a bit stone, a little more after Christmas and a little less in the summer, and because he trains either very early morning or very late evening there's never been much pace or structure to his running. Three years after getting into a regular running pattern, his 10k PB is just over the hour. So, out of Jim and Rachel, who's the advanced experienced runner?

What I'll say, therefore, is that if you have the will to do so, are in good general health and can do some sort of planning, prioritizing and add in a small measure of bloody mindedness, you should be able to find the time to do the Improvement schedule below. How fast you will do these runs will vary substantially, based on factors such as age, gender, weight for height, body fat percentage, natural 'talent' level – not omitting the mental aspect of how hard you wish to push yourself. I'd say that anyone who can run or jog continuously for 45 minutes can start to move onto this sort of schedule which, at least in the early weeks, is only a very gradual advance from the level they have already reached with their running.

The evolution towards the Progression plan is not that vast so, again depending on where each individual fits in the spectrum of endurance history, 'suitability' and commitment, there is no particular time frame for moving to this next level. It also doesn't make any allowance for the benefits of any other aerobic cross-training that may be taking place alongside the running, which will have some effect on building the runner's aerobic and cardiovascular fitness.

We'll use these sort of pace guidelines, so that:

- no one needs to become a slave to the stopwatch or Garmin unless they really wish to monitor at this level of detail;
- we can cater for a wide range of actual paces. For reasons described above,

there will be readers whose effort at 7 minutes per mile is the same as those doing 10-minute miling. Indeed, there will be guys who do sub-5-minute miles at the same level of effort but they will mainly be natives of Kenya and Ethiopia and just about getting by without this particular publication (more's the pity);

• we can keep to the same levels of perceived effort, and gradation of paces, as your aerobic fitness gradually improves.

The schedules use the following shorthand:

E – Easy, a pace whereby you can talk comfortably. Likely to be around 65–70 per cent of maximum heart rate.

S – Steady, a pace at which you can talk but it becomes slightly more challenging. Typically high 70s per cent to about 80 per cent of maximum heart rate.

T – Lactate turnpoint (threshold in old terminology). This is the pace you can maintain in an all-out effort for about 45 minutes and would be low 80s per cent of maximum heart rate. For many runners it is fairly close to 10k race pace. Coaches who are keen to stress the positives about structured running describe this as the fastest pace at which you remain comfortable, while a more forgiving coach would be more inclined to view this as when it just begins to get uncomfortable.

R – Repetitions. Let's call this your 20-minute race pace, so it's clearly going to be quite tough, at about 90 per cent of maximum heart rate. If you have just 20 minutes to give your all, and you are trying to do this at an even pace, then after 3 or 4 minutes at the right level of intensity your breathing will be at an intensity that will restrict any chat to fairly rushed half sentences.

I – Interval. This is hard and fast; it will be at about 100 per cent of your velocity at your maximal oxygen uptake, or vVO_2 max. It's about your notional 1-mile race pace, or 2k race pace, so within about 3 minutes of starting this sort of effort it will be extremely hard work, pushing up to mid-90s per cent of maximum heart rate, even higher if you are going right to your limits. Hence when you train at this sort of pace, which won't be on an all-year-round regular weekly basis, the bursts will be fairly short, with a recovery long enough to enable you to repeat the effort. Do be aware that interval training is not, either technically or metabolically, sprinting. Sprinting is your absolute maximum speed, so, give or take, what you can muster for about 15 to 20 seconds. Interval training is clearly a sub-maximal speed. Put more simply and generalizing somewhat, as you get fitter aerobically the difference between your interval speed and your sprint speed should become narrower.

Typically you should find that the sort of difference between each of the paces in the above 'degrees of difficulty' is about 20 to 25 seconds per mile. There's no need to agonize over the exact numbers session by session, whatever the level of complexity of Garmin you may be using, but do try to be aware of the clear difference of perceived effort as you move between the different paces.

The weekly mileage below is of course not an exact amount but it is broadly calculated on the basis that the runner has about 9 minutes to 9 minutes 30 seconds per mile as their steady pace, and that they do a proper 10- to 15-minute warm-up before their faster harder sessions and a 5- to 7-minute cool down jog after these structured sessions. Obviously at this level of volume and frequency the mileages aren't vast but you can clearly see how things evolve over the cycle and how every four weeks there is a back-off week to consolidate the gradual build-up in the previous three weeks.

It's worth doing some regular strides as part of a steady run and as part of a warm-up before the faster running sessions. By 'stride' we mean an effort of about 10 to 12 seconds at about your notional 800m to 1500m race pace ('notional' unless you have chosen to get embroiled in middle-distance running, which most road runners won't do). This pace and duration is long enough to recruit your fast twitch fibres, long enough to give you some strides to practise focusing on some technical points below, but not so long that you become anaerobically fatigued (which would happen if you extended this pace up to, say, 40 seconds and beyond), nor so long that you can't maintain full mental concentration on good technical form.

If you wish to build these programmes after doing them for a couple of sixteen-week cycles but wish to keep your focus on 5k to 10k races, think about applying the following progressions within the four-runs-per-week structure:

- Gradually extend the long run so that three weeks in every four you are running up to about 90 minutes.
- Raise the intensity of the later stages of the long run so that for perhaps the last 20 to 30 minutes you are running at about notional half marathon race pace – or about 30 seconds per mile slower than 10k race pace.
- Include some hill interval sessions along the lines described below. Try an eight-week block in which you do about six structured hill sessions, but not more than one per week, and do these instead of an interval session, not in addition to it in the same week.

A DO'S AND DON'TS CHECKLIST FOR STRIDES

DO	DON'T
Head and chin up, jaw relaxed	Clenched fists spreading tension up the body
Shoulders relaxed, low and pulled back	Rounded back either tilting back or over-leaning forward
Arms loose and floppy, 90-degree bend at elbow	Hips and pelvis rolling with each stride
Torso, erect, slight forward lean	Tight shoulders
High hips, bottom tucked under	Arms crossing over in front of body (lateral movement)
Leg movement focused on pushing off not pushing down	Heel strike (breaking effect)
Toes pointed to shins ('dorsi flexion')	Overstriding
Cadence – fast shorter strides, aim for 180 strikes/90 steps per minute at race pace	

- Slightly reduce the recovery time between efforts at interval or repetition pace. As your cardiovascular efficiency improves you should find that the pace can be maintained if you chip away at the recovery time, but don't 'lose' more than about 30 per cent of the recovery shown in the sessions above, or you will be unlikely to maintain target pace. For example, if you have used 2 minutes' recovery, don't go below 80 seconds' rest.
- Add about 10 minutes to the fourth weekly run.

Intervals

When you wish to progress the challenge of an interval session, then you can alter any of the following aspects of it:

- Increase the number of repetitions.
- Increase the duration of the repetitions.
- Decrease the recovery time between repetitions.
- Increase the intensity of what you do during the recovery bouts.
- Be mindful that you can only amend the nature of an interval session so far before you start to alter the nature of the training stimulus. For example, if you wish to do about 12 minutes of running at very close to 100 per cent of your speed at VO_2 max, a session of 8 × 90 seconds with 90 seconds' walk recovery should be manageable. As you get fitter you might well be able to do ten reps of 90 seconds at the same pace, or keep the number of efforts to eight but reduce the recovery to 60 seconds. But if you tried to do sixteen reps of 90 seconds, with just 45 seconds' recovery, which is most definitely a valid but tough session for the right runner at the right stage, the overall average pace,

relative to your speed at 100 per cent of VO_2 max, would need to be slightly lower.
- As a general guideline for runners newer to interval training, it is changing (or increasing) the pace or intensity of the recovery that is the deceptively difficult one to master. So, for example, if you change your recovery from a walk or very slow jog/shuffle to a quicker jog of maybe 10 minutes per mile/ 6.35 per km, you will definitely notice how it starts to bite. If you wear a heart rate monitor you will notice how a more dynamic recovery results in a much gentler decline in the heart rate. Indeed, if you want to make these intervals really bite and are astute on pace judgement, you can experiment with what has been termed Lactate Shuttle, or New Interval Training, or simply Fast Recovery. For example, for a 43-minute 10k runner, the session might be 8 × 2 minutes at 5k race pace, so about 6.35 or 6.40 per mile, with 2 minutes' semi-recovery at 7.45 to 8 minutes per mile. This is deceptively hard, probably right on the line of what this level of runner could manage. During the bouts of semi-recovery, the pace is still sufficiently high that the heart rate and blood lactate will stay fairly elevated.

An ideal off-road softer surface.

THE TRAINING PLANS

Plan 1: 4 Runs Per week

	MONDAY	TUESDAY	WEDNESDAY	THURSDAY
WEEK 1		35 Easy	warm up – 30 Tempo – warm down	
WEEK 2		35 Easy	warm up – 5 × 6 Tempo (90 sec rest) – warm down	
WEEK 3		40 Easy	warm up – 4 × 5 min R (2.5 jog) – warm down	
WEEK 4		35 Easy	warm up – 20 Tempo	
WEEK 5		40 Easy	warm up – 35 Tempo	
WEEK 6		40 Easy	warm up – 8 × 3R (2) – warm down	
WEEK 7		warm up – 5 × 7 Tempo (90) – warm down	40 Easy	
WEEK 8		35 Easy	warm up – 25 Tempo	
WEEK 9		warm up – 5 × 5R (2)	40 Easy	
WEEK 10		warm up – 12 × 80 sec 1 (80 sec and 3 min jog between sets)	40 Easy	
WEEK 11		warm up – 7 × 4R (2) – warm down	45 Easy	
WEEK 12		35 Easy	warm up – 30 Tempo	
WEEK 13		warm up – 40 Tempo	45 Easy	
WEEK 14		warm up – 6 × 5R	40 Easy	
WEEK 15		warm up – 5 × 8 Tempo (2) – warm down	30 Easy	
WEEK 16		warm up – 3 × 5R (2) – warm down	30 Easy	warm up – 15 Tempo

FRIDAY	SATURDAY	SUNDAY	TOTAL MILES
40 Steady		50 Steady	19
40 Steady inc. 6 × 20 sec strides		55 Steady	20
25 Steady + 8 × 11 (60 sec jog)– warm down		55 Steady	21
25 Easy		45 Easy	15
warm up – 2 × 6 × 11 (1 min/3min jog between two sets) warm down		60 Steady	20
40 Steady		65 Steady	22
warm up – 3 × 5 × 11 (1, and 2.5 jog between each set of 5) – warm down		65 Steady	23
30 Easy inc 6 × 20 sec strides		50 Steady	17
50 Steady inc 6 × 20 sec strides		70 Steady	24
warm up – 4 × 9 Tempo (2) – warm down		70 Steady	24
warm up – 40 Tempo		75 Steady	26
25 Easy inc. 6 × 20 sec		55 Steady	17
warm up 2 × 6 × 1.51 (1.5 and 3 jog between sets) – warm down		70 Steady	25
30 Steady then 15 Tempo		70 Steady	25
20 Steady – 8 × 11 (1) – warm down		55 Steady	23
		10K race	19

- There are endless options to this sort of session and the key is to be solid with the pace of the recovery rather than push the pace of the faster stints. Do the maths and you'll see that these sessions are relatively short. They are, for 5k and 10k types, clearly race-specific, so I suggest using them as part of a balanced programme but not doing them excessively if you are racing on a weekly or fortnightly basis.

If you ever overcook an interval session so that the overall target pace becomes unsustainable because the early pace has been too quick, I suggest that once the pace drops by more than about 25 to 30 seconds per mile you should end the session and try to complete it in full on another day. Physically and mentally, if you are trying to do a fast session at about your notional 3k race pace, then trudging round fairly short reps at slower than 10k race pace is of negligible additional benefit to the stimulus that the early overzealous reps will have triggered.

Fartlek

Many readers will know that this is a simple but effective training session, originated in the 1940s by Swedish middle-distance runners who were then setting world records. It means literally 'speed play' and in its pure form was done over fields and country with runners varying the intensity as they wished and simply managing the effort according to how hard a session they planned at that stage and on that day. Obviously something as basic as that can be used effectively and enjoyably by runners anywhere.

My only advice is that if you plan to do a fartlek session, do structure it so that you are doing what makes sense in your training plan, and keep an element of variety in what you do. So, for example, if you train with a group who have done a measured session of 15 × 400m on a Tuesday and do a fartlek two or three days later, don't base it around faster efforts in that 60- to 90-second range or you are broadly replicating what you have

Speed endurance in the city, parachute optional.

just recovered from. Also, be honest about the level of intensity you cover through the session. An easy 6 miles with ten efforts of about 15 seconds towards the next lamppost (lampposts have acquired an almost iconic status in fartlek running) is technically fartlek but it won't be a tough run.

Interestingly the Kenyans use the word 'fartklek' to describe any interval or threshold session done in the natural environment rather than at the track. (They refer to track sessions as 'track', so no training secrets there.) Their group fartleks are notoriously hard and long and often a matter of attrition, with athletes doing as much as they can for as long as they can before jogging the rest of the route.

Pyramid sessions are possibly a middle ground between precise interval sessions and random fartlek. So, for example, a session of efforts of 1–2–3–4–3–2–1 minute with a 90-second to 2-minute recovery would have similar demands to an interval session based around 400m to 800m reps, while a longer session of say 6–7–8–7–6 minutes with a similar recovery of about 90 seconds would be working more around the runner's anaerobic threshold/lactate turnpoint. Broadly speaking, the most successful runners tend to use fartlek in training when they are not in the specific build-up for a target race. You can become more precise as the key race approaches, and decide how rigid you wish to be when planning your training.

Hills

The aerobic challenge and benefits of hill sessions will be in line with the gradient, duration and intensity of how you run up, and indeed down, them. The options of structured hill sessions are quite literally infinite so there is no magic or 'correct' session; it will depend on what the challenge is intended to be. For the statistically inclined, there are tables which show the conversion of what a given pace up an incline is 'worth' if done on the flat. I have seen many hundreds of detailed training schedules of élite runners and not one has ever found it necessary to record their actual speed uphill. Very broadly, the sort of gradient that most hill sessions would use results in about a 25 per cent loss of speed versus running on the flat. The loss of speed obviously becomes greater as the gradient increases, and it is a slightly exponential rather than linear trend. In practice, a calibrated treadmill would be the way in which the exact gradient would be measured.

Don't lose sight of the fact that, if you are preparing for a fairly flat road race, charging up and down hills is part of the means to that end, not the actual goal. Avoid hills where the gradient is so severe that it forces significant changes in your running movement and also slows down your cadence. Such steep hills do of course benefit your cardiovascular system, your strength/strength endurance and your co-ordination (and indeed if you ever venture into fell or hill races then they become part of your specific training), but it's more specific to develop these capacities using movement patterns closer to what you are preparing for. So seek gradients roughly between about 4 per cent and a maximum of 7–8 per cent, and don't worry if the gradient varies within the stretch of hill that you are using.

Downhill, Too

As Isaac Newton would have noted if he'd spent more time at undulating road races instead of lobbing apples through the air, what goes up also comes down, so remember that running downhill fast isn't yet banned by Health and Safety factors. International coaching guru Jack Daniels says: 'Most runners

Heading downhill in a cross-country race....

underestimate downhills, as they generally don't provide much of a challenge to negotiate.' British endurance legend Eamonn Martin, former UK record holder at 10,000 metres, advises: 'Downhill running requires a forward lean, which requires less energy. Most runners going downhill lean backwards and arch their backs, which puts the brakes on. By increasing the loading through their legs, they slow down. Some of it is psychological as athletes are scared they may fall over, but they very rarely do.'

For the statistically minded who wonder why a hilly course doesn't, on the stopwatch, balance the slower pace uphill with the accelerated pace downhill, there's clearly a limit to the cadence, stride length and biomechanics that a runner can deploy doing downhill,

...or uphill in a road race.

which goes nowhere near matching the loss of pace that a steep and/or long ascent will cause. The compensation factor has been shown to be about 55 per cent.

So, how to cover both uphill and downhill benefits in a session? As an example, if you have a long hill or a hilly loop you can do both short and long reps on the same circuit. So, say there is a 4-minute uphill effort at something like 5k race intensity. The downhill jog would probably take a similar time or slightly longer, with gravity assisting of course, but how about putting a 40-second burst about half way downhill. That way each loop comprises a 4-minute climb and a 40-second faster stride downhill. Three to five of these loops would be a good, relevant session.

Extending the Programme

So, with these progressions taken on board, you might end up with a twenty-week programme that looks like the plan below. Twenty weeks is broadly in line with a half-year or seasonal macrocycle, once factors like end-of-cycle breaks and transition back to regular structured training have been factored in. A fifth weekly run is added in to make a clearer difference in load between this and the previous programme. If your preference is to stick to four runs a week but still increase the load, I suggest that you add about 15 to maximum 20 minutes to two of the other weekly runs, but don't 'trick' yourself by simply extending the warm-up or warm-down duration – that simply adds junk miles but doesn't add a noticeable training purpose. Once a warm-up or warm-down has been done to make you 'fit for purpose', it's done.

The race frequency is just a guideline; many athletes will run significantly more or less than the quoted four races in twenty weeks. I suggest you have at least one race

Those who like to race frequently should ensure adequate periods of recovery.

in the build-up so that you are physically and mentally attuned to running right to your limit on the day. Some people can do this in training, but most people find a small extra margin of effort in a race environment, so it's worth practising. Others find the time, enthusiasm and commitment for much more frequent competitive tests. That's also fine – ultimately it's your leisure time to derive maximum enjoyment from.

Try to avoid over-racing. Firstly, the intensity of a race run to the limit will require a period of recovery, whatever the distance, so the more you 'race yourself fit' the more you risk some level of burnout or lack of training variety. Secondly, you may slip into the 'next week' syndrome. It's anecdotal rather than based on the profundities of sports psychology, but if you are racing nearly every week you can slip into the habit of always giving about 95 per cent and never 100 per cent – stepping off the gas slightly when it becomes really tough in the later stages, because there's always next week to pull out all the

stops. If you really like to race frequently, do at least pick out a smaller number of target races with the others acknowledged as secondary tests, where you may not taper the running to squeeze out that extra couple of per cent.

The schedule below doesn't embrace racing goals beyond 10k, but there wouldn't be a problem in trying a 10-mile race off this sort of build-up. Indeed, many thousands of people have tackled and survived half marathons with a less demanding and less structured training plan than this, though I suggest that if you ran a half marathon off this schedule the last three miles or so could be particularly difficult. Scaling down the distances, 5ks are fine as periodic race options, as is the ever-increasing range of park run options. They are short enough, and of course always happen at nine o'clock on Saturday mornings, that an easy longish run the next day is still an option for many. Other shorter races are also more widely available in the midweek during summer, when the evenings offer more daylight. Do dip into

Plan 2: 5 Runs Per week

The plan below builds logically and, I hope, manageably, from the previous schedules for those who wish to push things just a little further in terms of frequency of runs, length of runs, and intensity of the harder sessions. It is in the realms of 30 per cent more demanding than the previous plans and could act as a bridging stage between the earlier plans and a more full-on 'harrier'-type schedule, where the runner is expecting to run five or six days per week and typically heading out the door for at least 45 to 50 minutes on virtually every training session.

	MONDAY	TUESDAY	WEDNESDAY	THURSDAY
WEEK 1		40 Easy	warm up – 30 Tempo warm down	
WEEK 2		40 Easy	warm up – 5 × 6 Tempo (90 sec rest) – warm down	
WEEK 3	35 Easy	40 Easy	warm up – 4 × 5 min R (2 jog) warm down	
WEEK 4		35 Easy	warm up – 25 Tempo – warm down	
WEEK 5	35 Easy	45 Easy	warm up – 8 Tempo (90 sec) – 2 × 6 × 30 sec hills (jog back and 2 min jog between sets) – warm down	
WEEK 6	30 Easy	35 Easy	warm up – 8 Tempo (90 sec) 2 × 7 × 30 sec hills (jog back and 2 min jog between sets) – warm down	
WEEK 7		35 Easy	warm up – 4 × 9 Tempo (2 min rest) – warm down	30E
WEEK 8	30 Easy	warm up – 8 Tempo (90 sec) – 2 × 8 × 30 sec hills (jog back and 3 min jog between sets – warm down		45 Steady
WEEK 9	35 Easy	warm up – 8 Tempo (90 sec) – 3 × 6 × 30 sec hills (jog back and 2 min jog between sets) – warm down		warm up – 5 x 7 Tempo (90 sec rest) – warm down
WEEK 10		warm up – 2 × 8 Tempo (90 sec – 4 × 21 (90 sec) – warm down	35 Easy	

FRIDAY	SATURDAY	SUNDAY	TOTAL MILES
45 Steady		65 Steady	24
45 Steady inc. 8 × 20 sec strides		70 Steady	26
30 Steady + 10 × 11 (60 sec jog) – warm down		80 Steady	30
35 Easy		60 Steady	20
warm up – 5 × 7 Tempo (90 sec rest) – warm down		65 Steady	29
30 Steady		5k or 5 mile race	21
warm up – 15 Steady – 12 x 11 (1 rec) – warm down		80 Steady	29
warm up – 10 Steady – 30 Tempo – warm down		85 Steady	31
45 Easy		80 Steady	31
20 Steady – 5 Tempo 10 easy		10k Race	22

Plan 2: 5 Runs Per week (continued)

	MONDAY	TUESDAY	WEDNESDAY	THURSDAY
WEEK 11		40 Easy	50 Steady	warm up – 9 Tempo (90 sec) – 2 x 9 x 30 sec hills (jog back and 3 min jog between sets) – warm down
WEEK 12	35 Easy	warm up – 6 x 4 R (2) – warm down		warm up – 12 Tempo (2) – 10 x 90 sec 1 (90 sec jog) – warm down
WEEK 13	35 Easy	warm up – 8 Tempo – (90 sec) – 2 x 9 x 30 sec hills (jog back and 3 min jog between sets) – warm down		warm up – 4 x 10 Tempo (2) – warm down
WEEK 14	35 Easy	warm up – 2 × 7 x 90 sec 1 (60 sec/3 min jog between sets) – warm down		warm up – 15 Steady – 25 Tempo – warm down
WEEK 15	30 Easy	warm up – 2 × 7 Tempo (90 sec) – 2 x 4 R (2) – 5 x 11(1) – warm down		30 Easy
WEEK 16		warm up – 5 × 8 Tempo (2) – warm down	50 Easy	warm up – 4 x 4 R (2) + 10 x 11 (1) – warm down
WEEK 17		warm up – 25 Steady – 20 Tempo – 5 Easy	45 Easy	warm up – 2 x 6 x 21 (70 sec/3 min jog between sets) – warm down
WEEK 18		warm up – 7 x 4 R (2) – warm down	35 Easy	5 Easy – 25 Steady – 15 Tempo – 5 Easy
WEEK 19		warm up – 3 x 7 Tempo (90 sec) + 8 x 1.51 (1) – warm down		10 Easy – 20 Steady – 15 Tempo – 5 Easy
WEEK 20		warm up – 2 x 5 R (2.5) – 5 x 11 (1) – warm down	35 Easy	

FRIDAY	SATURDAY	SUNDAY	TOTAL MILES
	40 Steady	80 Steady	31
40 Easy		85 Steady	31
40 Easy		90 Steady	32
45 Easy		70 Steady	31
25 Steady – 4 Tempo – 5 Easy		5k or 5-mile Race	23
	40 Easy/Steady	90 Steady	33
35 Easy		85 Steady	32
50 Easy		75 Steady	33
35 Easy		65 Steady	25
25 Easy – 3 Tempo – 5 Easy		10k Race	20

these, and adjust your schedule accordingly, so that you aren't, for example, doing three sessions or races at the same pace during a seven-day period. The long run in the 80- to 90-minute range doesn't have to be confined to the weekend; for many it can be accommodated, with a bit of planning, around a day's work.

Mix and Match

One coaching point to consider is that a runner may be keen to do both some harder running within a club or group structure whilst also closely adhering to a relevant training plan either individually provided by a coach or a sensible generic schedule. Nothing is set in stone and there's more than one way to skin a cat. So if your schedule calls for, say, sixteen reps of one minute on the evening when your club is doing 20 × 200m at the track, or 12 × 400m, then physiologically we are in the same ball park, albeit you may may be slightly diluting the planned progression within your own plan. If, however, those 400m reps are in place of a session of 5 × 7 minutes at about your 10k pace, then that's a fairly different training stimulus. Your training plan may well have somewhere else in the week a similar type of session to what the club is doing, so try to avoid too much repetition in your repetitions, as it were. Many running clubs now preview their main group sessions on the club's webpages, typically posting then in monthly blocks, so runners and indeed coaches and run group leaders can make good use of this in their planning.

Young Runners

Some readers may have children or even younger siblings who are showing some enthu-

siasm for distance running, and the results of park runs show a few early teenagers chancing their arm at 5ks. That's fine as far as it goes, and given all the frightening data about childhood obesity and inactivity we should surely not be discouraging youngsters from some purposeful endurance running. Indeed, the sort of training plans shown above wouldn't be out of place for a keen youngster with a couple of years' training aged perhaps 15 to 17, or indeed older if they are progressing with it and have no wish to push things further. However, be aware that the best training for teenagers usually isn't doing exactly the same as adults. If you are rearing or related to an early teenager – or indeed pre-teen – who likes the sport, by far the best long-term pathway for them would be the sort of training and racing that has been offered within the 'traditional' athletics and harriers clubs across the country. It's the pathway that has brought through Paula Radcliffe and Mo Farah, so it has some tremendous credentials underpinning it, albeit each coach will work to his or her own individual style.

The vast changes in the sport in recent decades now mean that many keen and talented youngsters may end up not in a buoyant athletics club but in a long-distance road-running club, with most people having had no experience of the sport as a youngster. Of course, many youngsters drop out of the sport, as has always been the case, but as parents, coaches or run leaders we owe it to them to at least give them a good grounding in athletics and athleticism rather than immersing them into long distance from the outset (and 5k and 10k are long distance, don't doubt that). There are some highly respected books for training younger distance runners. Indeed, running 5ks and even 10ks won't do mid-teens and older teenagers any harm at the upper end of their racing plans, but do be cautious about how you might apply these training principles to young athletes.

Treadmill Quirks

Many treadmill users wonder about the differences there may be between real outdoor running and running on a moving belt where however far you go you don't go anywhere. Metaphysics aside, most runners are aware that setting the gradient at 1 per cent is very close to replicating the air resistance of outdoor running. Running on a treadmill at zero

A road race finishing at the track.

gradient gives a slightly flattering pace, by about 6 to 10 seconds per mile.

Detailed studies at the University of Pennsylvania analyzed runners' movement patterns at a range of typical running speeds and at both flat conditions and on a steep uphill gradient (10 per cent) and similar downhill gradient. Interestingly, when this research was done, in the early 1970s, the leading exercise physiologists weren't expecting to see any significant differences between a runner moving forward over firm ground and a runner moving nowhere but doing the run over a moving surface. The running speeds tested were 4.20 per mile, 6.30 per mile and 8.20 per mile. Few readers will be operating that faster pace for any sustained efforts but you are likely to be very familiar with the other paces, and indeed may do regular speed interval sessions at somewhat quicker than 6.30 pace.

Broadly, the tests showed that at 8.20 miling there were very few significant differences between 'real' and treadmill running. However, as the pace picked up, the trend was that the stride lengthened on a tread-

mill, there was slightly less vertical velocity on the treadmill, and there was a slightly longer support phase (i.e. ground contact time) with the quicker paces on the treadmill. The cause and effect chain seems to be that running on a treadmill produces a lesser movement in the centre of gravity compared to running over the ground. This leads to the runner placing the lead foot further forward from the centre of gravity, whilst the moving belt returns the supporting foot beneath the body. This results in the longer support phase, the slightly longer stride length and, it follows, slightly lower cadence.

What does this mean in practice for runners and coaches? Probably not a vast amount. It ties in with my experience that the one type of training that one very rarely finds being done on a treadmill is the quicker intervals (the pace where the mechanics become most different) as done by top-flight runners – less than helpful for a national level 1500m athlete. But away from that 'niche' user, there does not seem to be any other performance or injury or efficiency discrepancy between running over a moving or a still surface.

CHAPTER 4

AEROBIC CROSS-TRAINING

Aerobic cross-training is in a separate chapter from the strength and conditioning chapter because the content in this section is related to activities which can in some way replace or replicate the benefits of running training, while the strength and conditioning elements are aspects that support and supplement the running.

With the main element of your running being cardiovascular efficiency, it is logical that any activity that can challenge you in a similar way to running is of some use. The world of cross-training and how it crosses over with running has changed considerably in the last twenty or thirty years, with these various factors all contributing:

- The growth of triathlon, so that many runners split their sporting loyalties between cycling and swimming as a matter of course and their running performance will always have some short-term or longer term cross-training programme supporting it.
- The growth of gym culture, so that many new runners enter the sport from a medley of cross-training modules via their gym, particularly steppers, spin bikes, elliptical trainers. With no background in a 'traditional' running environment they have evolved their running as part of a broader aerobic programme.
- Arguably there is a less hardy approach to running 'in all weathers' so that, linked to the growth in gym membership, runners may more readily trade a run for a cross-training session when the weather outside is particularly bad. In the depths of winter this may be good common sense and an injury avoidance technique that some hardened harriers might consider.
- There is greater precision and empathy in the sports medical world, so that whereas in bygone years the advice to an injured runner might be to stop running and do a suitable remedial set of conditioning drills, nowadays there will be a more specific and runner-friendly approach to what aerobic training can be carried out while the running is on the back burner.
- The increasing use of the internet and social media has made more recreational runners aware of how élite endurance athletes may incorporate cross-training into their running build-up, either as a regular integral element or more usually as a way of rehabbing an injury without compromising aerobic fitness.

As with all aspects of training, you'll need to work out what best suits your own particular circumstances and level of commitment. Don't lose sight of the importance of event- and sport-specificity. If cross-training was completely transferable across sports then in theory a Tour de France cyclist should be able to crack out a 2.15 marathon and the mighty East African half marathon élite should be able to hop on a bike and demolish the cycling world in a 1-hour road race.

Anyone who saw how hard the USA cycling legend Lance Armstrong had to work just to sneak under 3 hours in a marathon will see my point.

Conversely, one of the GB marathoners selected for the Olympic Marathon in late August 2004 spent about ten weeks in the middle of what would have been the specific build-up unable to run because of injury. In this ten-week spell the athlete largely mirrored what would have been the duration, heart rate and intensity of her running training by using an elliptical cross-trainer and spin bike. The injury gradually cleared in time to do a short spell of key running sessions and the athlete had a fine result in Athens.

A case of what might have been? Maybe in part, but also a reflection that the aerobic quality of the non-running training was thoroughly planned with the Athens goal in mind, and the runner was clearly highly motivated to train hard towards that goal. Plus there would have been a large amount of running 'carry forward' from the training that the athlete had done in preparation for the London Marathon in April 2004, which had secured the Olympic selection.

This chapter will not address in detail how cross-training can be used to keep fit while too injured to run, as that will vary case by case according to the nature of the injury and in light of individual medical advice. Rather, it looks more generally at how the various options may work for you.

The overarching premise should be that your training for running should optimally be running. When, for whatever reason, you adopt aerobic cross-training, you should aim to keep two or three key sessions each week as running sessions to maximize the specificity of the training stimulus; the cross-training should mainly be used as additional basic, steady state work.

Some scientific research on this subject has looked at fit, well-trained runners in the 18- to 19-minute range for 5 kilometres and had one group add three runs to their weekly training, while the second group added the same duration in three cycling sessions. The improvements in 5k results after two months were very similar in both groups, which endorses the benefits of aerobic cross-training, but it's worth emphasizing that in this research both groups did their more intense sessions as running throughout the period.

With all cross-training done indoors, be aware that the lack of any air resistance, often coupled with a higher air temperature than outdoors, will lead to a far higher loss of sweat than doing the same session outdoors. About one litre of fluid and electrolyte replacement per hour should be taken on board ideally during the session and topped up promptly after finishing, when you will probably continue to sweat at this increased rate for some minutes.

UK Athletics in recent times has moved towards recommending cycling rather than an elliptical cross-trainer for when its élite endurance runners deal with injury. This is perhaps counter-intuitive as one would see the cross-training movement as closer to normal running than cycling is – if nothing else, you don't sit down to do it. However, the rationale is that the higher cadence of cycling and the smoother, more forward-driving cyclical movement is a better means of preserving running efficiency than the clunkier movement of the cross-trainer. Of course, the cardiovascular benefits of both options are governed by the intensity of the effort.

Cycling

Typically, 1 mile of cycling at a given intensity or heart rate is 'worth' about one-quarter of a mile of comparable running effort in aerobic benefit. This means that to match the training effect of a 1-hour run, very roughly, you may need to cycle between 90 minutes and 2 hours, depending on your running level versus your cycling proficiency. This is a combination of the fact that cycling uses fewer of your total muscle groups than does running, and also any slight downhill on the bike means you may almost be freewheeling, whereas a greater effort would be needed to run at even pace down the same descent. This 'equation' is one reason why a typical triathlon programme will have much more time spent on the bike than on running.

Runners doing hard sessions on a bike, even a stationary bike, will invariably find that at high levels of effort, including absolute maximum, they will have heart rates about five to seven beats per minute lower than when running at the same perceived effort. This is partly because of the fewer muscle groups engaged as mentioned above, and also because whereas a trained competitive cyclist will have developed the powerful leg muscles to drive the bike at maximum cardiovascular effort, a 'mere' runner's legs will not be as specifically prepared to divert so much energy through the upper legs.

Elliptical Cross-Trainer

This is a fairly close replication to running with the great advantage of having no impact. The distribution of effort across the body's main muscle groups is very close to that of running. Using your preferred combination of heart rate or perceived effort, you can carry out any number of training sessions from an easy pace through to aerobic power work at your 3–5k notional race pace effort. It is harder to go at a higher effort than this as runners' biomechanics and the structure of the machine seem to prevent the rapidity of movement

needed to get the heart rate towards its absolute maximum. Perhaps because there is no impact, you may find when doing interval or repetition sessions that the recovery you need between reps is slightly less than when you do comparable running sessions.

Aquajogging/Water Running

The dual title for this activity is intended to show that it has a serious and useful benefit for improving performance and needn't be simply a base-level aerobic activity. Running in water provides a no-impact workout that exercises the same muscles as if you were running on land. It is tiring and, unlike normal running, it is much easier to lose your balance in the water. Keep in mind that you will get tired faster doing this than doing normal running because each stride is against the resistance of water.

Deep water running takes place in a deep pool without your feet touching the bottom, floating in place with the help of a flotation belt. Because the feet don't touch the ground, deep water running is completely non-impact, making it perfect for those with vulnerable knees. For a proper deep water exercise, lean slightly forward in the water, avoiding a straight up-and-down posture that won't give the workout its full impact as it will bring in assisted 'bobbing' movement due to the belt's buoyancy effect. Also avoid the lower leg (i.e. below the knee) coming forward past the knee – a movement which may occur in the water but is not how you would run on land.

Shallow water running involves a regular pool, with the feet actually touching the bottom. Because of this, it is slightly higher-impact than deep water running, but still much lower than traditional running. With feet making contact with a surface, the shallow water option more closely resembles normal running. As such, it is helpful for increasing running speed and strength. The exercise is done in much the same way as in deep water, but because your feet are making contact to help propel you forward it is often done somewhat more slowly. If you are using a heart rate monitor, expect that for a given rate of effort your heart rate will be about 5–10 per cent slower than in normal running. This is partly because in land-based running a proportion of the energy output is expended to deal with the shock of impact on each stride.

The less appealing factor about water-running is that the total door-to-door time required to do a session is much longer than doing a comparable running session. If you have access to a swimming pool at a work-based gym then this can help on the time management side. Mentally, of course, the four walls of a swimming pool tend to be less varied and stimulating than even a fairly humdrum running route, so you will need to form some sort of mental distraction to make sessions less boring. Doing intervals or fartlek or at least varied efforts helps with this: as well as heightening the aerobic training stimulus, it ensures that not every minute is exactly the same as the preceding and succeeding minute. There are also some organized coached groups doing structured water-running sessions, although these are relatively few at the current time.

Swimming

The big advantage of swimming is that there is no impact, so the risk of running injuries is negligible. The downside is that the transferability of swimming fitness to endurance running is generally less than that provided by the other cross-training options. The cardio-vascular element is of course excellent and, generally, can be as hard as you wish to make it provided you are able to swim continuously, so it works well as a maintenance option. But naturally the muscle groups used in swimming, and the way they are used, vary significantly from those used in running.

Another possible limitation is that to provide a structured aerobic session, as opposed to just continued lengths at a steady state, one does need a certain level of technical proficiency to be able to swim at a relaxed, slow effort when, for example, a recovery training session is planned, or if an interval session is planned with varying paces. As evidence for the importance of technical competence, the British Triathlon Federation's élite talent programmes will focus on youngsters with a swimming and running background where the skill can be taught young, and to a high level, whereas cycling can be moulded on later. In his coaching manual-cum-autobiography, triathlon legend Scott Tinsley describes seeing a lean, fit young man spluttering through swimming 25-metre lengths at over 40 seconds each and exclaiming, 'What the hell? I'm a 2.27 marathoner!' For those runners who do have a good level of swimming technique, one advantage is that they can carry out hard, structured training which, although it may be fatiguing in terms of aerobic challenge, doesn't produce that muscular wear and tear in the legs that comparably tough road or track running sessions will cause.

Rowing/Indoor Rower/Canoe Ergo

The widespread availability of indoor rowers, usually the Concept 2 machines, has kept rowing in the forefront of cross-training. Indeed, indoor rowing now exists as a sport in its own right, with various competitions available.

It is technically quite easy to master the indoor rowing motion to a level of competency that lets it serve as a cardiovascular element of one's running training. The simplicity of the movement, provided you are doing it with the lower back and hamstrings correctly positioned and correctly used, and the fact that the machines are invariably set up with computers to indicate speed and distance, along with sensors that monitor your heart rate, means that any sort of interval or repetition session can be done on a rowing machine in addition to continuous steady state training.

Less widespread is the canoeing world's equivalent of the indoor rower, where a simulated canoe paddle is used as the main tool of resistance with the athlete sitting on a machine which otherwise closely resembles a Concept 2. The same sort of training points are applicable here, with the added factor that the paddling movement is slightly more technically precise than ploughing ahead on the rower. Currently these items are about triple the cost of indoor rowers (hence they are less widely available), but they serve a useful aerobic purpose.

Rowing and canoeing place great emphasis on upper body strength and endurance, far more than does endurance running – the body shape of high level athletes in these sports shows this clearly. So the transferability of the training benefit is not as high as cycling or the elliptical provide. The London Marathon performances of the likes of Steve Redgrave and James Cracknell prove the point.

Triathlon Crossover

Triathlon has grown hugely in recent years at every level. There are now extensive fixture lists across the country covering a range of distances and options across the swim/bike/run disciplines. At global élite level, the diversity of nations with high performers is continually expanding from when in the 1980s it was largely a USA and Australasian monopoly centred around sunny beach cultures. The depth of competition is now immense – as I write, an athlete I coach has placed thirty-first in the national age group championships, just 3 ½ minutes behind the winner in 1 hour 57 minutes of racing!

The reality for most coaches is that if they coach a number of runners, they will inevitably coach people who are actually runners and triathletes. So, what difference does it make to the training and performance? We won't go into any details on biking or swimming here – that's for those sports' specialists. We'll just consider briefly how much of a performance trade-off there may be in training purely as a runner versus a comparable balanced triathlon programme. Every case history is its own story and set of data, but the general impression is that the percentages to be gained from a single-sport specifics may be less than people expect.

We can start at the very top with 2012 Olympic Champion Alistair Brownlee. His typical training load is in the region of 30 hours per week. The split is very roughly 25 per cent swim, 50 per cent bike, 25 per cent run. Off this, the world's highest achieving triathlete programme, he can run very close to 29 minutes. He and his coach, who both have extensive roots in UK distance running, have predicted that if he spent twelve to eighteen months focusing solely on his running (and the 2014 Commonwealth Games was mentioned as a possible running target at the time of writing) he would be looking at about 28 minutes or slightly over – so, a major revamping of his training would gain him about 3–4 per cent on the watch in his running. That's very much in line with the sort of experiences I have seen – guys running 3.10 marathons off Ironman training nip under 3 hours when they focus on marathon specifics, and 35-minute 10k runners within triathlons head towards 33 minutes if they prioritize the running. Bear in mind that the context here is that the level of commitment and intensity remain constant. For a newer, lightly trained triathlete evolving over some years into a more full-on runner, the performance gains would be much greater.

So the general message here for recreational runners would be to encourage regular swim and bike training and triathlon competition, combined with regular running training, if that is what you enjoy. With all the other variables and immeasurables, the difference in running performance if the training loads are broadly comparable will not be vast.

CHAPTER 5

RUNNING MOVEMENT SKILLS

The Principles

When endurance coaching gurus are asked to put into a single sentence what they would seek to instill in any successful runner, they invariably make reference to having sound technical running form. This is because in terms of efficiency of movement, or the biomechanical aspect of 'running efficiency', this will enable the runner to cover the distance quicker. It will also usually be linked to a lower incidence of injury.

That's the simple part. The more difficult part is analyzing what comprises sound technique, applying it to each individual runner, and then the runner spending the necessary time developing the best technique possible.

Let's be realistic and accept that among the many reasons people become involved in long-distance running, practising running drills is very rarely part of the attraction. The busier you are in your life, the more you will want to prioritize your training time on doing the running rather than doing the activities that support the running.

But reflect on what you are trying to achieve, both in the running and the supplementary training. If you isolate one tough training session in a five-month block of preparation – let's say six reps of 5 minutes at about 10k pace with a 60-second jog recovery – how much actual impact on performance does that one session have amidst what may be well over 100 running sessions? Not

The 2004 Olympic Marathon champion, a study of great movement.

Concentrate on two or three coaching points for each drill.

much, but it is hard work and will take an hour or so of your time, all told. What if you spent one hour broken down into four blocks of 15 minutes, during each of which you spent quality time developing your running technique along good biomechanical lines? Would the benefit be any more or less than the notional rep session?

We don't know exactly, but one thing we can identify from watching élite endurance runners is that almost without exception they move efficiently. How they have developed this ease and grace of movement will vary immensely, and indeed there will be an element of genetic luck in their body type and their musculo-skeletal structures. There will be athletes who as children were well taught in running movement years before they ever had a focus on distance running; others who may have had some specialism in other sports involving running, been coached within that particular sport and later transferred this skill into distance running. To some extent these are the lucky ones who have benefited from what we can call either 'transferable skills' or 'invisible training' and their endurance training as adults is in some ways simplified.

For others, the pathway may be less gilded as we have to play catch-up for the skills we have not had so well embedded in earlier years. The general guidelines for practising these sorts of drills include:

*   Try to focus on two or three key movement points on each drill; any more than this and it's hard to give due concentration to what you are trying to achieve.
*   Do each drill for about 8–10 seconds, regardless of how many reps you do in this time or what amount of ground you cover. Again, this is related to concentration levels and also to avoid any signs of fatigue creeping into the movement pattern and compromising whatever is your best attempt at it.

Try to keep the upper body in optimal running posture when doing drills, not looking down.

- Two or three reps per drill will be enough to help embed the technique – both left and right sides where applicable.
- Don't do the drills after a long run or hard session when you will already be fatigued; after a comfortable, paced run of about 40–45 minutes they should be able to be carried out efficiently.
- Do a thorough warm-up before doing these drills so you aren't going into what are challenging movements or positions without preparing the muscles and joints accordingly.

There is often an element of self-consciousness that many distance runners will have to overcome to do these drills, particularly if they are doing them on their own and away from a track-based group where the drills will be seen as normal behaviour.

Whatever your actual level of movement skill, you will only be able to perform the drills as well as your overall strength and conditioning allow, so there is a substantial tie-in between these elements of supplementary training. The current trend seems to be that core strength and core stability are now part of many runners' training, whereas the movement training is much more rarely integrated. It's true that you will find runners up to a fairly high level who don't move especially well and who don't address this in their training. Rather then showing that this is an optional add-on, I suggest instead that these runners would, all things being aerobically equal, perform better if they spent some time sidelining some of the easy mileage and using the time to improve their technique.

The Running Movement Cycle

The following section is included to give readers some knowledge of exactly what happens to your body when you run and so provide a logical basis for the strengthening, conditioning and technical elements of training that you may carry out. The text isn't a means of self-diagnosis for any injuries you may pick up. However, at some point in your running progression you are likely to suffer an injury and whoever treats the issue should apply a

Drills can aid running technique.

Creative ways to help speed and coordination.

more detailed version of this biomechanical knowledge to help you address the cause of the injury. This should reduce the likelihood of its recurrence and thus link into improving your running performance.

The relationship between biomechanics and injury is specific to each body part. Overall, though, poor mechanics of any body part will either increase the landing forces acting on the body or increase the work to be done by the muscles. Both increase the stress, which – depending on the individual and the amount of running – can become excessive and cause injury. For readers wishing to delve into this aspect in further detail, there are some recommended books listed under 'Further Reading' at the back of this book.

Running can be seen as a series of alternating hops from left to right leg. The ankle, knee and hip provide almost all the propulsive forces during running. The running cycle comprises a stance phase, followed by a float phase where both legs are off the ground.

At running speeds that correlate with most runners' training and racing paces, a single running cycle will take approximately 0.7sec, out of which each leg is only in contact with the ground for about 0.2sec.

It is, not surprisingly, during the stance phase that the greatest risk of injury arises, as forces are acting on the body, muscles are active to control these forces, and joints are being loaded. There are two parts to the stance phase. First, the 'absorption' or the 'braking' phase. The body is going through a controlled landing and the foot rolls in to absorb

Keep good posture when doing drills.

impact forces. At this point the leg is storing elastic energy in the tendons and connective tissue within the muscles. Next is the 'toe off', when the foot leaves the ground as part of the 'propulsion' phase. The ankle, knee and hip all push the body up and forward, using the elastic energy stored during the absorption phase.

This is an efficient way for the body to work. The more 'free' recoil energy it can draw from the bounce of the tendons the less it has to make or draw on from its muscle stores. Research shows that at least half of the elastic energy comes from the Achilles and foot tendons.

Ankle, Knee and Hip Mechanics

At initial contact there is flexion in the ankle, the knee and the hip. The further forward the trunk leans, the greater the hip flexion. If the gluteal hamstrings are not actively pulling the foot backwards, then the foot contact will be too far ahead of the hips and the braking forces on the leg are increased.

During the absorption phase the ankle and knee flexion is coordinated to absorb the vertical landing forces on the body, which at typical distance running speeds are about two to three times bodyweight. This is why eccentric strength in the calf and quadriceps muscles is required to control the knee and ankle joints and manage the braking forces, otherwise the knee and ankle would collapse or rotate inwards.

During the second half of the stance phase the ankle, knee and hip combine in a triple extension movement to provide propulsion upwards and forwards. The calf, quadriceps, hamstring and gluteal activity during the propulsion phase is less than during the absorption phase, because the propulsion energy comes mainly from the recoil of elastic energy stored during the first half of stance. During the swing phase of the 'flight' the knee and hip reach maximum flexion and then re-extend with the ankle dorsiflexing.

Good runners will follow these movement patterns. It is essential that the ankle and knee can quickly control the braking forces and create a stable leg system to allow the tendons to maximize their recoil power. Too much upward bounce will increase the landing forces, putting greater stress on the joints and requiring more muscle force to control. Runners need to learn to bounce horizontally and not upwards, by taking quick, light steps.

It is also important to bring the foot back as this reduces braking forces and the time needed for the absorption phase. Good strength in the gluteals, hamstrings, quadriceps and calf muscles will help runners achieve this.

In summary, excessive braking forces can contribute to injury. The correct movement patterns of the hip, knee and ankle combined with correct activation and strength of the major leg muscles will help control braking forces.

Pelvis and Trunk Mechanics

At initial contact the trunk will be flexed forward slightly and there is a slight fowards-leaning tilt. This slight forward flexing of the trunk during the braking phase helps to maintain the body's forward horizontal momentum. Gluteals, hamstrings, abdominals and erector spinae (stabilizing muscles in the back) are all active to control the trunk and pelvis during the absorption phase.

During the propulsion phase the trunk re-extends to the initial position. This slight shift in the anterior (frontal) tilt of the pelvis helps to direct the propulsion forces of the leg horizontally.

In summary, a slight forward lean and anterior pelvic tilt is thought efficient for running. Too much forward lean may suggest that the posterior (rear) chain muscles (hamstrings, gluteal, erector spinae) are not strong enough and this may increase the strain on the hamstrings and back during the running action. Too upright a posture may encourage vertical movement, which will increase landing forces.

An excessive tilt during the propulsion phases is normally associated with tight hip flexors and inadequate range of motion during hip extension. This will reduce the power of the drive from the hip and encourage a compensatory reliance on lumbar extension.

In general, a poor trunk position or lack of pelvic stability is likely to reduce the efficiency of the running action, creating extra load on the leg muscles or increasing stress through the lumbar spine and pelvis. Any of these negative factors can increase the likelihood of injury.

The pelvis and trunk during stance phase should be stable and provide balance. The gluteus medius muscles (abductors) are important in providing lateral stability: their eccentric contraction before and during the absorption phase prevents the hip from dropping down too far to the swing leg side. An excessive or uncontrolled pelvic tilt increases the forces through the lumbar and sacroiliac joints, and forces the supporting knee to internally rotate, which in turn may increase the forces on the ankle. There is often a correlation between excessive pronation and excessive pelvic tilting in runners, and it is a good illustration of how one unstable link in the biomechanical chain can have an adverse knock-on effect and increase the risk of injury.

Foot Mechanics

The outwards and inwards rolls of the foot during running are called supination and pronation. This rolling action is normal and healthy. It is only excessive pronation or supination that leads to injury.

At initial contact the foot is in a supinated position. During the absorption phase the ankle is dorsiflexing, which naturally also causes the foot to pronate. This allows the foot to be flexible and absorb the impact forces of landing.

At around mid-stance the foot begins to supinate. This moving of the foot into a more rigid position allows for a stronger push-off and more efficient recoil through the foot and Achilles tendon. You can feel the difference for yourself: roll your heel and ankle inwards and your foot will feel soft and flat. Then roll your heel and ankle out, and your foot should feel strong with an arch.

Pronation and supination both involve complex three-dimensional movements of the heel, ankle and tibia. The normal trend is for the inversion (inwards-facing) angle and the eversion (outward-facing) angles to be around 5 to 10 degrees.

Analysis of these movement patterns can

Note the slight forward lean of this Italian runner.

lead to runners being recommended to use orthotics, but this should be done as part of a more holistic movement analysis. Runners' mixed responses to orthotics is linked to the complexity of the movements involved.

An excessive supinator will typically land with the foot inverted and then it remain inverted during the stance phase. This means that they will lose out on the shock-absorbing benefits of the normal pronation movements. Excessive supinators tend to suffer from injuries to the lateral knee and hip, and can also be prone to stress fractures because of the higher repetitive impact forces.

If a runner spends too long in pronation, the foot will not be in a strong position to assist push-off during the propulsion phase, so the lower leg muscles will have to work harder. Excessive pronators tend to suffer from anterior knee pain, medial tibial stress syndrome, Achilles and foot soft-tissue injuries.

Upper Body and Arm Mechanics

The main function of the upper body and arm action is to provide balance and promote efficient movement. The arms and trunk move to oppose the forward drive of the legs. During the braking phase, the arms and trunk produce a propulsive force and during the propulsion phase the arms and trunk combine to produce a braking force. This pattern reduces the braking effect on the body and so conserves forward momentum.

As the right knee drives up and through in front of the body, the left arm and shoulder move forwards – counteracting the knee motion. The normal arm action during distance running involves shoulder extension to pull the elbow straight back; then, as the arm comes forward, the hand will move slightly across the body.

The arm action also contributes to the lift during the propulsion phase, which may help

Which top level runner better balances the need for power vs efficiency at the end of this 10k race?

the runner to be more efficient, reducing the work done by the legs.

Barefoot Running

One recent hot topic is the supposed merits of barefoot running. The arguments, simplified, are as follows:

- Many runners' feet are poorly conditioned for endurance training – a combination of the sedentary lifestyle most people now lead, combined with the highly over-protective, cushioned, heavy training shoes now produced. Using our weakened feet to do extensive road running (or, in most cases, pavement running, an even more unforgiving surface) we just compound our weaknesses, running inefficiently and becoming injured.
- Our ancient ancestors were hunter-gatherers, apparently living a quasi-endurance lifestyle by chasing animals just to keep themselves alive. They did this barefoot.
- Certain types of shoes are now available to educate our feet muscles and tendons to more closely replicate this natural movement and that by doing selected bouts of barefoot running on suitable surfaces we can assist this process.

Supporters of this argument often quote the legendary Ethiopian, Abebe Bikila, who won the Olympic marathons in 1960 and 1964 without shoes, and the naturalized British runner of the 1980s, Zola Budd, who also ran barefoot in her heyday, having toughened her feet from infancy in rural South Africa. However, the overwhelming majority of élite long-distance runners, close to 100 per cent, do use training shoes, even on soft surfaces, and when poor young East African runners are trying to make a breakthrough in their training

approach they will clamour for running shoes if they cannot otherwise afford them.

While all the comments about our weakened feet sound sensible, the allusion to our supposed ancestral endurance lifestyle is somewhat inaccurate. Prehistoric man hunted in short sharp bursts. Even if it did take many hours or even days to catch the hunted animal, this was not endurance running in any sustained form but a series of unstructured shorter bursts with long breaks. There are no prehistoric hunters' training diaries yet available, but hunting was done on much softer surfaces than pavements and tarmac.

The prominence of this debate has been raised immensely in the last two or three years, with a combination of journalists, shoe manufacturers and certain 'barefoot coaches' seeming to be in the forefront of the 'movement' along with sports scientists. Arguably it has taken on a life of its own rather than being seen as an integral part of an athlete's running movement, which is itself closely linked to that runner's strength and conditioning status.

Or look at it another way. If you read the training histories of the greatest runners – the people for whom running is most central because it is their means of livelihood and, in the developed world at least, the runners who have the most cutting edge support systems in sports science and medicine – very rarely do barefoot running or minimalist shoes feature in their or their coaches' thinking. What they do focus on are the factors that collectively create a robust, well-conditioned, efficiently moving athlete.

One of the more objective sources of useful information is the Harvard University website dedicated to the theme. Amidst a wealth of academic research it offers some helpful 'Tips on Transitioning to Forefoot or Midfoot Striking'.

Forefoot striking barefoot or in minimal footwear requires you to use muscles in your feet (mostly in the arch) that are probably very weak. Running this way also requires much more strength in your calf muscles than heel striking, because these muscles must contract eccentrically (while lengthening) to ease the heel onto the ground following the landing. Novice forefoot and midfoot strikers typically experience tired feet, and very stiff, sore calf muscles. In addition, the Achilles tendon often gets very stiff. This is normal and eventually goes away, but you can do several things to make the transition successfully:

- **Build up slowly.** If you vigorously work out any weak muscles in your body, they will be sore and stiff. Your foot and calf muscles will be no exception. So please, don't overdo it because you will probably injure yourself if you do too much too soon.
  - Start by walking around barefoot frequently.
  - First week: no more than a quarter of a mile to 1 mile every other day.
  - **Increase your distance** by no more than **10 per cent per week**. This is not a hard and fast rule, but a general guide. If your muscles remain sore, do not increase your training. Take an extra day off or maintain your distance for another week.
  - **Stop and let your body heal if you experience pain**. Sore, tired muscles are normal, but bone, joint, or soft-tissue pain is a signal of injury.
  - **Be patient and build gradually**. It takes months to make the transition.
- If you are currently running a lot, you don't need to drastically reduce your mileage. Instead, supplement forefoot or midfoot striking with running the way that you normally ran before beginning the transition. Over the course of several months, gradually increase the proportion of fore-

foot or midfoot striking and reduce the proportion of running in your old style. Use the same 10 per cent per week guideline to increase the amount of running you do forefoot striking.

- It is essential to **stretch your calves and hamstrings** carefully and regularly as you make the transition. **Massage your calf muscles and arches** frequently to break down scar tissue. This will help your muscles to heal and get stronger.
- Listen to your feet. Stop if your arches are hurting, if the top of your foot is hurting, or if anything else hurts! Sometimes arch and foot pain occur from landing with your feet too far forward relative to your hips and having to point your toes too much. It can also occur from landing with too rigid a foot and not letting your heel drop gently.
- Many people who run slowly find that forefoot striking actually makes them run a little faster.

Using the old-fashioned method of pen, paper, mental maths as taught in the late 1970s and an optional anorak, I have calculated how the mileage would build up using that 10 per cent weekly increase guideline, with a starting point of 1 mile four times per week – the maximum recommended as the day zero baseline. After 13 weeks you have built up to a still modest 12.6 miles, but interestingly, and perhaps encouragingly, after 26 weeks the weekly barefoot mileage is a handsome 46 miles – and the likelihood is that very few readers of this book are averaging more than 46 miles per week of running. It's also notable that the numbers and the caveats coincide very closely with the one detailed case history that I have coached (we linked up after he had made the transition), and the athlete is now running PBs of 35 minutes for

10k and 59 minutes for 10 miles with training of around 50 miles per week. In his case, we have found that doing the easier runs in barefoot sandals while wearing racing shoes for the faster efforts and runs is a healthy balance, as he has slightly more protection when he is generating a higher impact. He has also tried to shift more of the running away from pavements to trails and paths, though not always in the winter.

At the risk of sounding cynical, nearly all the most vehement proponents of barefoot running are those with something to sell: primarily shoes of course, but also books, running lessons or niche coaching qualifications that don't yet have any governing body accreditation in any sport.

One of the most authoritative voices on this subject is leading British podiatrist Clifton Bradeley, formerly a sub-4-minute miler, who has spent the last twenty-five years professionally working with sports people's feet and movement patterns. His view is, quite simply, that if we were meant to run barefoot we would have been doing it a long time ago. 'The notion that the cave man would run a barefoot marathon everyday to gather food is not correct; we evolved to hunt as a group at speed over short distances,' he says.

As for forefoot running, Chi and POSE running, again Bradeley is very cautious. Eighty per cent of runners run heel to toe. The view is that by trying to alter this gait through specific drills or by purchasing special

SOME FURTHER POINTS TO CONSIDER ABOUT BAREFOOT RUNNING

- Every person is individual and what works for one does not work for all. Not all runners need to strike on their forefoot to be the most efficient runners. For many runners at their normal training speeds, rearfoot striking is actually the preferred manner of running.
- Trying to make someone who is naturally a rearfoot striker into a forefoot striker may injure them.
- A runner who is a rearfoot striker at 10min/mile pace may be a forefoot striker at 5min/mile pace. Remember: running speed changes your foot strike pattern. For endurance runners this may prompt a revisiting of the notion of a universal 'best practice' model. Top-level 1500m runners will race at a speed not that far removed from their full speed – perhaps 14 seconds per 100 metres with their maximum sprint speed typically just under 12 seconds per 100 metres. The comparable level at a marathon would be about 18 or 19 seconds per 100 metres, so the biomechanics and need for power versus economy of stride are different. The same principles will apply to runners of less exalted standard, maybe even more so because they are likely to have a greater differential between their maximum speed and their long-distance race pace.
- Running barefoot strengthens the postural muscles in the feet and lower leg, if these have previously been neglected by underuse and/or heavily cushioned shoes.
- Running barefoot/minimalist increases proprioceptive (spatial) awareness and balance. This should result in a slight improvement on running efficiency.
- Running barefoot/minimalist forces a change in mechanics to adapt to the forces on the feet.
- There are as yet no clinical trials that show the effect of barefoot running for a prolonged period of time.
- There are currently no research studies that prove that wearing traditional running shoes increases injuries or that barefoot/minimalist running reduces injuries (and vice versa).

equipment (Newton shoes, for example) we massively increase our risk of injury. This is because of a concept called asymmetry.

Years of research and practice have convinced him that the key to efficient and successful running performance comes from the pelvic position and its relation to the upper and lower body. Hip height and leg length discrepancies can play havoc over long periods of sustained running on flat, hard surfaces as the body tries to compensate, causing excess pronation and postural changes. 'Ninety-five per cent of non-traumatic sports injuries can be put down to body asymmetry,' says Bradeley, who believes that effective shoe design and the use of orthotics is the only way to effectively control this over the long term.

In Japan, 283 élite athletes had their foot strike recorded by high speed video at the 15km mark of a half marathon. A large majority, 75 per cent, were heel strikers. Less than 2 per cent (just four out of the 283) were forefoot strikers.

If you are progressing with your running, already including some drills that focus on speed and efficiency of movement and are largely free of significant injury, and are doing this in traditional shoes, don't necessarily assume that a transition to radically different footwear will be beneficial for you.

In summary, if you are considering switching to a more 'minimal' running shoe, do some further reading around the subject and ensure you follow a gradual transition programme.

Barefoot running shoes.

CHAPTER 6

FLEXIBILITY, STRENGTH AND CONDITIONING

The contents of this chapter are linked to the detail of Chapter 5 relating to the biomechanics of running movement. To move optimally at your target running speeds, you need to be flexible enough, strong enough and powerful enough to do so without becoming injured, using as little energy as you can.

Flexibility

This is invariably one of the hot topics in any discussion about injury prevention and running technique. Despite various pieces of research in recent decades, there is not yet any totally consistent approach within the sport on the merits of static stretching for endurance running.

If we look at the range of flexibility needed for long-distance running, it is clearly a smaller range of movement than is needed for 400-metre running, which is itself a narrower range of movement than is required for 110-metre hurdles. Of course, if we watch a mid-pack distance runner, particularly in the later stages of a race, we may see a cramped, shuffling style showing limited range of movement, particular from the waist down. This will be a visibly very different movement from how Mo Farah will blast round the final lap of a 10,000-metre race in 53 seconds. So we would make the easy, and at least partly correct, judgement that the slower runner

lacked flexibility and the simple recommendation would be to 'do more stretching' or, in some cases, 'start doing some stretching'.

In this context of relevant flexibility, each muscle has an optimal length whereby on contraction it can produce its maximum power – this is its 'torque'. Beyond this point, increased flexibility – manifested in greater muscle length – reduces power and thus negates performance. In terms of injury prevention it is strength more than flexibility in a muscle that is more relevant. The muscle's

Stretching with stable running posture.

63

eccentric strength is its capacity to resist lengthening and the length/power balance is what is important in the muscles used in running.

That said, many runners may indeed have limited flexibility for what is needed for their events at their target pace. This may particularly be the case with veteran runners, where the natural default is to experience a reducing range of movement with increased age.

When warming up before a race, bear in mind that there is no valid evidence that static stretching in the warm-up phase either assists better performance or prevents injury. Indeed, if you do a significantly different routine from what you do in your warm-up for training sessions, you may actually worsen your performance by putting your muscles through unaccustomed movements and your body temperature may go down rather than up. This race-specific scenario is mentioned because training sessions may, in reality, be slightly rushed, whereas the extra time that a runner may have allowed to arrive at a race venue may lead him or her into thinking that 'more is better'. For the range of movement that you will deploy in a race of 5 or 10 kilometres, it is unlikely that you need to do any additional static stretching. Your 'fit for purpose' state can be achieved by a build-up of easy and steady running, some skipping for both height and length, and some faster strides at about your target race pace or slightly faster.

The above comments should not be confused with a stretching programme that has been advised by a medical practitioner, where specific areas are shown to lack the required range of movement for the runner's purpose, resulting in an injury.

When researching this book, I checked the advice on stretching in other running publications and there is no particular regime that is consistently backed up by research. Some writers suggest, simplistically, that it is unlikely to do you any harm if you at least maintain

Lateral movements have a place in a warm-up.

your range of movement, and combine this with what seems logical based on observation. There is at least medical support to actively avoid restricting one's flexibility. In *The Complete Guide to Stretching*, physiotherapist Chris Norris states 'when the full range [of extensibility and elasticity] does not occur, the muscle can shorten permanently and alter the function of a joint'.

Strength, Strength Endurance and Power

The English Institute of Sport, the pan-sport agency that helps prepare élite athletes in over thirty sports, describes its approach to strength and conditioning as based on 'optimizing the body's force, power and velocity capabilities specific for the athlete and the event'.

In applying this for endurance runners, there are some proven research findings:

- In 1999 controlled tests showed that 5k/10k runners who completed a nine-week programme of explosive strength drills improved performance more than those who did no such resistance training. The improvements were shown not to have been derived from additional advances in either VO_2 max or lactate threshold compared to the control group, but from progress in running economy and neuromuscular adaptations.
- In 2000 further research showed that improved running speeds were based on achieving greater ground forces, and that the limiting factor in this is the time available to exert one's force, rather than the maximum force itself. Put simply, it is more about power (the speed at which strength is utilized) than about maximum strength itself.

The key to developing power for running is one's elasticity. Only about 50 per cent of the energy produced by oxygen during aerobic running is actually used to fuel the muscles' movement forwards. About 5–10 per cent is used in shock absorption and about 10–15 per cent is needed to overcome air resistance. About 40 per cent is stored within the muscles and is available for their elastic capability. Of this 40 per cent, half is channelled below the knee to the Achilles tendon and the arches of the feet.

Moving from the scientist's outlook to that of the endurance coach, George Gandy, former UK Athletics Endurance Head Coach, describes the need 'to develop strength for force in the propulsive muscles and for tolerance of stresses by equally attuned non-propulsive elements. Sufficient freedom of joint movements must also be ensured so as best to apply these forces, and enough specific endurance to allow the process to be repeated as often and as quickly as required'.

So, in practice, and without the benefit of an expert strength and conditioning coach to give you an individualized programme, do try to focus on development of power rather than strength itself so that the challenge is specific to what your running progress requires.

Bear in mind that this is very much a means to an end and you are just trying to make yourself 'fit for purpose'. A shot putter or sprint hurdler might expect to see some direct links between what they can achieve in weight training and how this translates to their target event, whereas a long-distance runner would be less likely to see such a clear link.

However, runners are only as strong as their weakest link. We can illustrate this by two examples, both fairly typical in the current running environment. Firstly, a male, mid-30s, who has played rugby and cricket through school, university and club level, with regular coached training sessions in both sports. Fairly new to any endurance sport, although he also keeps up a simple weekly gym session from what he recalls of his rugby conditioning. He is a 45-minute 10k runner and wishes to break 42 minutes for the distance. So he isn't yet looking to run especially quickly, and he brings a historically well-conditioned frame to his current running level.

Contrast this with a female of similar age, who was never involved with sport at school but who has belatedly found her niche in distance running, now covering 60 miles weekly and looking to break 37 minutes for 10k. To do this, she'll need to be doing some training and racing at significantly faster than her target 10k time, at maybe 5min 30 per mile or just over 80 seconds per lap of a 400-metre track. If she has no conditioning background, either for running or another sport, then her aerobic and cardiovascular level may be well in advance of the underlying strength, and she carries a high injury risk.

The classic analogy is that of a motor car's chassis and engine. Our hypothetical ex-rugby player needs to build up his engine within a strong chassis, whereas the speedy woman needs to ensure her chassis is strong enough to withstand the velocity that her engine makes her capable of generating and sustaining.

As guidelines on how to fit strength and conditioning (S+C) sessions into your running programme, consider the following:

- Even at very high levels there is not universal agreement amongst coaches and athletes on how close to the competition phase one should maintain an S+C routine. But bear in mind the overarching principle of specificity – doing a set of lunges, step-ups and dead lifts on a Tuesday before a 10k on the Sunday certainly won't contribute

to a new PB on the day, though it might make a contribution towards making you more robust to tackle further training once you have recovered from the race. The typical trend would – as logic suggests – involve more frequent S+C in the general training phase, and less in the specific event preparation. This would be broadly the opposite to how the running load changes.

- Try to avoid doing an S+C session within about 4 hours either before or after a running session if at all possible. There is a theory that this causes an 'interference effect' that results in both the aerobic and the strength session being somewhat reduced in their effect. There have been numerous research projects to try to establish a clear rationale on how to manage this, but the results are not conclusive. It is acknowledged that in reality, when people sometimes have just one training window in a day, the sessions may have to follow one another. And indeed many very good club groups have a regular structure of doing an easy or steady run and then proceeding directly to some sort of strength/strength endurance session. There is a logic that if a strength session is to be done at a challenging level of resistance, being fatigued at the start from a tough aerobic session will not enable you to perform as you would wish in the strength session, and one would not find good athletes going from a tough interval or threshold session to a meaningful resistance session (though they may do so later in the same day).

- Do allow at least 48 hours, or two nights' sleep, between conditioning sessions. If they are challenging enough to be of benefit then you will need at least a day of recovery and absorption before taking up the challenge again.

Pilates

In recent years the growth in popularity of Pilates, and its application for distance running, has brought it to the attention of many runners who have included it in their conditioning programme. In the UK one of its leading proponents in athletics has been Joe Mills, a former national 1500-metre champion and sub-4-minute miler who has worked in the Canadian high performance system. He summarizes the aspects where Pilates can bring benefit as follows:

- Ineffective muscle use — specifically, losing the correct and optimum balance between the mobilizing muscles and the stabilizing muscles.
- Faulty recruitment patterns — muscles work in groups to achieve the optimal and most economical movement patterns and typical sedentary lifestyles tend to result in deviations from the optimum. So runners will adopt inefficient recruitment patterns in their running and these become embedded as the norm, unless something is done to remedy them.
- Neutral pelvis and spine: these form the body's axis from which all movement stems, so the two aspects above need to be rooted in a strong, well aligned spine and pelvis. This is why all Pilates sessions start with the requirement to establish, and be able to feel, what comprises neutral.
- Joints: once one has lost ideal posture and muscle balance, the impact forces through activities such as running will not be so fully absorbed through the central — and strongest — section of the affected joints. Over time this is likely to lead to excessive wear and tear around the joint with ensuing higher risk of injury. For the runner,

this will typically relate to knees, hips and ankles.
- Breathing: there is an intrinsic link between the muscular efficiency around the core, which is of course where all the respiratory organs are located, and the 'quality' of the breathing itself. As endurance running performance is related to the amount of oxygen taken in and used around the body, breathing inefficiencies will impact adversely on performance.

Do be aware that Pilates may not meet all a runner's strength and conditioning needs, depending on where each runner sits on the balance between strength and endurance. Also, many drills that one encounters in a Pilates session have been absorbed or transferred across to other regimes that may be called 'core strength', 'core stability' or 'body conditioning'. So, for example, many runners will do exercises commonly called 'Crab', 'Plank' or 'Bridge' without ever having

This focuses on lower back, hamstrings and gluteals.

For strength and stability in the abdominals, gluteals and quadriceps.

Strength and balancing exercise for lower back and abdominals.

This leg extension drill works the hamstrings, hip flexors, gluteals and abdominals.

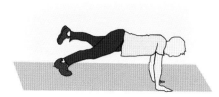

The much-used Bridge works the back, abdominals and gluteals.

Abdominals, gluteals and lower back are worked in single leg extensions.

The famous Plank and its variations engage the black, gluteals and abdominals.

Hip-flextor muscles are tested in this side stretch, as are abdominals.

attended a Pilates session. But if your core is fit for purpose you probably aren't too concerned about who 'invented' the system you are tapping into.

Pilates can therefore benefit the runner through low threshold recruitment of the deep abdominal muscles, improved posture, efficient breathing and the importance of correct neutral alignment during functional movement. It is possible that a regular set of drills rooted in Pilates principles, combined with structured hill-running sessions, may meet most or indeed all of your conditioning to make you fit for purpose for your running goals.

In Practice

All this material about torque, energy return, mobilizers and stabilizers might leave you wondering what level of sophistication need go into your own sessions. Be assured that there is a large amount you can do that may well be familiar from general circuit training.

As an example, the large and successful Birmingham University endurance squad, whose recent athletic alumni include World Championship marathon runner Dave Webb and World 1500 meters silver medallist Hannah England, have a regular weekly circuits session based around the following. The structure is that three sets of all drills are done, with the effort vs recovery split being about 25 seconds of work with 10 seconds of recovery and transition. It's worth noting that the abdominals have a variety of drills so that there is a more widespread development of muscles around the core area, and not just an unhelpful isolated focus on a six-pack surrounded by relatively weaker muscles. The duration of the session is designed to give a suitable balance of strength endurance for endurance runners, so it isn't an aerobic training stimulus.

Hip flexor circuits:

- high knees
- split jumps
- single leg squats, left and right
- lying down on side, side leg raises, left and right
- lunges front
- lunges backwards

LEFT: Lunges, with slightly varying positions and grades of resistance, condition the gluteals, quadriceps and hip flexors.

RIGHT: The squat is the classic resistance exercise for all over conditioning. It engages the gluteals, quadriceps and hamstrings. It is fine for beginners to use bodyweight or very low extra weight. A straight back, correct positioning and movement are essential to reduce injury risk.

Abdominals circuits:

- sit-ups over knees
- feet together, side touches
- high reaches
- sit-ups, hands to opposite knee
- double feet up and out
- buttock to ankle touches
- leg shoot

Some similar benefits are achieved by what the aforementioned Gandy developed over many years at Loughborough University, which has been a hub of British élite endurance running for nearly forty years. The conditioning programme is perhaps simpler than you might expect given the scientific talk that underpins it. It includes:

- bounding
- press-ups
- squat thrusts

- chinnees (or chin-ups)
- hip thrusts
- skipping
- rope climb
- bent leg sit-ups
- Step-ups onto a 30cm step/box
- In addition, for a more advanced challenge, box jumping and rebounds can be added for a greater plyometric challenge, although this should be done only by athletes robust enough to do so as the injury risk is higher.

The structure of the session would be along the lines of thirty circuits of 30 seconds (maximum) with maximum of 30 seconds' recovery/transition, so a broadly similar strength-endurance focus to the Birmingham option. Nearly all of these can be readily carried out in one's own home if a gym isn't always accessible, although rope climbs will only be found in the more idiosyncratically furnished living rooms.

RUN FOR THE HILLS: ALL-ROUND TRAINING CONDITIONING

The following paragraphs show how hill training can be used to cover these training bases without necessarily being rooted in the finer points of exercise science.

Two examples of high achievers using short hills as their means of developing running power are: Eamonn Martin, former UK record holder at 10,000m (still third on our all-time lists) and the last British male winner of the London Marathon – with his trademark sprint finish in 1993; and Rob Denmark, Commonwealth 5,000m champion and the last British-born man to make the top 8 in Olympic and World Championships finals at 5,000m.

Both these runners had big sprint finishes to back up their huge aerobic capacity, yet both had a fairly simple regime of general conditioning exercises that most school PE teachers or a basic level personal trainer could advise on. Martin has described how he did some press-ups and sit-ups first thing in the morning while he waited for the kettle to boil, and indeed when in his later years the commercial returns on his running freed up a little extra time to start on a more robust weightlifting programme, there was not a discernible improvement in his running performance.

However, the major conditioning element that these athletes managed to gain from their running programme was the strength and strength endurance derived from short and quite steep hill repetitions. Both Martin and Denmark used a particular hill that took about 25 seconds to run up at high intensity, with a turnaround and jog back recovery of about 45 seconds. If you analyze the movement patterns involved in short hill bursts, you will see that they challenge and develop the key muscle groups used in some of the classic conditioning drills such as lunges, step-ups and half squats.

CHAPTER 7

INJURY PREVENTION AND MANAGEMENT

Overview of Overuse Injuries

Injuries are an inevitable part of running for most people. Before looking at the physical factors it's worth briefly analyzing the mental side of sports injuries, which has generated some sports science research in its own right. An injured runner is inevitably a less content person than an uninjured runner, and how we treat injuries will affect both our future running and, at least in the short term, our state of mind, so it's worth trying to make the most of whatever obstacles we have to deal with. Leaving aside élite professionals where a severe injury can threaten their financial livelihood, even committed amateur runners can place great store by their running, which is often linked to social networks, self-esteem, weight management and stress relief. With-

out our regular training 'dose' we lose much more than just the physiological effect of the missed training sessions.

To show the prevalence of running injuries, the following data was provided from over 200 runners in a London survey. The respondents represented a typical cross-section of long-distance runners, with over 95 per cent being in the 25–55 age group; 53 per cent running 20–40 miles per week; 14 per cent running 40–60 miles per week; 45 per cent with less than five years' running history and 27 per cent with between five and ten years' running on the clock. Clearly the table below is a summary, with no measurement of the injuries' severity, and in some cases such as 'knee pain' wrapping up a range of complex symptoms into a generalized category.

Condition	Percentage affected in last month	Percentage affected over running career
Knee pain	19	69
Ilio tibial band syndrome	8	58
Shin splints	3	42
Hip pain	13	40
Achilles tendonosis	6	36
Plantar fasciitis	3	30
Stress fracture	2	20
Piriformis syndrome	5	18
Other	9	47

If one takes a pragmatic view of these stats the percentages in the final column will inevitably rise as the runners' number of years in the sport increases. Suffice to say that sports medicine providers seeking to develop their understanding of running injuries are, quite reasonably, balancing the profession's Hippocratic ideals with good business sense.

While occasional impact or direct injuries can affect endurance runners – famous examples include Paula Radcliffe injuring a knee while signing her wedding invitations and Steve Ovett slamming his knee into some church railings while training – the vast majority of distance-running injuries are through overuse. Frustratingly, therefore, the running movement that builds up your fitness is the same running movement that may injure you.

Bear in mind that 'overuse' is a deliberately generic word that in running injury terms can simply mean 'too much' in the widest sense. Too much mileage per se, of course, but it can also include any of the following causes:

- too much running on pavement or tarmac
- too much running in inadequate shoes
- too rapid an increase in the volume of training
- too rapid an increase in the intensity of training, even if the volume has stayed the same
- too sudden a change in the training regime, whether related to the running and/or non-running elements of the training programme
- too much uphill or downhill running
- too much running on an uneven road camber
- too much training on an inadequately nourished or dehydrated body
- too much training on a sleep-deprived body
- too much running for the body's particular state of biomechanics.

That's a lot of factors so it's no wonder that so many runners suffer some sort of injury at some point. It does, however, back up the overarching philosophy of making training progress gradual rather than sudden.

Working with Medical Advice

If we exclude degenerative conditions such as advanced osteoarthritis, and trauma injuries which may permanently damage your musculo-skeletal structure, there really should be very, very few injuries somehow 'caused' by running that would need to end your running career. You may need to do extensive rehab exercises; you may eventually need to consider the benefits of minor surgery; you may need to be very careful about surfaces, very long distances, frequency of running or footwear; but one way or another there should be a source of treatment to enable you to carry on as a regular endurance runner.

The word 'conditioning' has just as wide a coverage. For distance running we could think of it in modern management speak as meaning 'fit for purpose'. There are élite runners whose 10k preparation may include up to 130 miles weekly on the roads; if they can sustain this without any of the above factors taking a toll, one way or another they have become adequately conditioned to do so.

The degree to which runners trust their medical advisers is key to the recovery process, and is linked to their diligence in following the recommended rehab programme. So, just as with your running, do set some goals and structure to your non-running recovery process. If your practitioner is as committed to eliminating and preventing the injury's recurrence as you are likely to be, there may be a regular and precise set of exercises and drills that you are advised to do. Two or three sessions per day is not uncommon from sports medicine specialists, maybe up to 40 or 50 minutes daily building up the conditioning needed to reduce the prospects of the injury recurring. This has the added benefit that mentally you will still have that structure and commitment to a training plan, even though it won't involve belting round your most scenic training routes.

When you decide that an injury does need some medical diagnosis and advice, take a pen and paper to your first appointment (which may be your only appointment, if you are lucky), ask your specialist the following questions, and note down and act upon the replies:

- What caused the injury?
- What exactly should I do to prevent the injury recurring?
- How often should I do the rehab exercises and how long should I continue to do them for?
- How long should I cease running for?
- When I start running, how should I build up the running duration and frequency?
- What cross-training options can I pursue in the meantime?
- Can I do these cross-training options with the same intensity as my running?

Your practitioner may not be able to provide all these answers, but it's definitely worth asking. Bear in mind that the healing process may vary in duration and that a second or in some case third appointment may also be recommended. It's an annoying scenario for any runner to be in – not only are you unable to run, but you are incurring extra expense in doing so and probably spending what would be training or leisure time in travelling to appointments and doing the recommended rehab. Do follow the rehab advice precisely as recommended, however time-consuming

and boring it may be. If you don't, you are more likely to be making recurring visits if the injury recurs.

There is a major link between the conditioning of runners, their biomechanics and their incidence of injury. So if you find that you increase your average mileage from say 25 to 35 over two months and become injured in doing so, on the one hand it may well be that the increased mileage partly caused the injury. On the other hand, don't take this to mean that you will repeatedly become injured when you run 35 miles weekly. It should be a matter of increasing the strength/strength endurance qualities of whatever caused the injury (quite often more than one factor is involved) so that you can in future withstand a higher training load, if that is how you wish to progress.

The often quoted guideline of avoiding mileage increases of more than 10 per cent per week has its general uses but it doesn't acknowledge that each runner will have an injury threshold, which will vary as their robustness increases or decreases. So if you are having recurring injuries, keep a tab on how your mileage has evolved and look for indicators of what may be your cut-off point.

Also, bear in mind that if the increased training creates an injury after months of pain-free running, the degree of 'fault' that needs remedying is probably not that vast because it has managed to get you through several months of decent training at a slightly lower level.

The consensus among sports coaches through recent decades is that sports medicine is becoming ever more widely understood and practised, and indeed medical students now have the option of pursuing sports medicine as their specialism at a much earlier stage in their careers than used to be feasible. Not surprisingly, many sports

Injury Type	Symptoms	Typical Causes	Possible Treatments
Achilles Tendonosis (inaccurately often described as 'tendonitis')	Pain on and around the Achilles heel area, particularly on rising in the morning and at the beginning of a run.	Tight calf muscles, over pronation and overzealous increase in hill training or faster running.	Calf raises to increase strength and mobility – rigorous progressive programme advised. Massage.
Ilio Tibial Band Syndrome (ITBS)	Sharp pain on the outer side of the knee as a result of the tendon becoming inflamed.	Any combination of overuse factors, particularly downhill running, pronation or tight lower leg and hip flexors.	Increase flexibility of tight areas; massage of ITB including self-massage with tennis ball or foam roller. Can be a very insidious problem to get rid of.
Piriformis Syndrome	Deep pain in buttock area, may be linked with painful stabbing feeling down hamstring if sciatic nerve compressed.	Any weakness or imbalance around major muscle groups in lower back, glutes, hip flexors or abductors or hamstrings.	Massage affected area and surrounds. If piniformis is in spasm, can be quickly released by external massage. Also use tennis or golf ball self-massage to stave off tightness.
Plantar Fascititis	Acute pain under front and middle part of foot, particularly on rising in morning. Caused by inflammation of the plantar fascia tendon.	Combination of overuse factors plus weak foot muscles or high arches.	Ice or contrast bathing (alternate hot and cold water for 5–10 min spells). Self-massage with golf or tennis ball. 'Night boot' also particularly useful to stretch out the plantar fascia and reduce pain in 7–14 days.
Runner's Knee (patellofemoral pain syndrome)	Stabbing deep pain around kneecap, particularly going downhill or downstairs.	Poor tracking of knee as it moves, related to imbalance or weakness in surrounding muscles and tendons, particularly vastus medialis, the inner quadriceps. Flat feet or weak pelvic area.	Strengthening relevant areas by single leg squats and step-ups onto chair or step.

Sciatica	Acute stabbing pain anywhere from the lower back, down through the glutes, hamstrings and the calf.	Any inflammation or displacement of the third, fourth or fifth lumbar vertebrae or of the first sacral vertebra (lower back, broadly), which presses on the sciatic nerve.	Combination of rest; anti-inflammatory treatment and physio/ massage to alleviate the area causing the pain (normally not the prime site of the pain). Also try – with care and correct technique – nerve stretches; the 'Slump' for the lower back; glutes and hamstrings, and 'Point and Flex' for where the nerve passes through the calf to the Achilles.
Shin Splints	Pain around the inner lower leg/shin. Can become acute quickly but can also disappear quickly after initial rest in early stages.	Combination of overuse factors cause inflammation of the medial tibia where the muscle meets the bone.	Massage the affected area, plus ice, plus anti-inflammatory gel. Avoid hard surfaces, overused trainers and downhills while recovering. Also strengthen calf and shin muscles.
Stress Fractures	Specific sharp pain, most commonly in metatarsals (feet and toes) and in shin. Also there is now a lower level 'stress reaction'. in layman's terms a halfway house, which needs to be rested for a much shorter timescale to prevent it from becoming a stress fracture.	Combination of overuse factors. Rarely show up on an X-ray so an X-ray isn't at all conclusive.	The recovery period seems in nearly all cases to be very close to six weeks and 'testing' the injury any earlier is very likely to cause a relapse. Avoid weight-bearing training during rehab period.

doctors are or were committed sports players so will share the runner's mindset about being motivated to get back into training as soon as possible.

There's no escaping the fact that, if you wish to be treated quickly, taking the private medicine route will invariably offer a speedier response than using National Health Service provisions, and experience suggests that you may receive a longer appointment slot for a more holistic diagnosis. However, there are sports medical practitioners who split their time between public and private systems, so don't assume you won't be offered a high level of technical expertise through the NHS.

Of course, the internet also enables us to take the riskier route of becoming our own physician by dialling our symptoms into a search engine and seeing what is the best diagnostic match. The great pluses of this 'system' are that it is free and easy to access and doesn't require you to sit in a doctor's waiting room flicking absently through glossy magazines. The obvious downside is that it offers less than 100 per cent reliability.

The large majority of all running injuries will fall within the issues described, in outline, below. You should also be aware of the anatomical links throughout your body, which mean that although you may experience pain at a particular place, the root cause of the problem may well be somewhere else in the body. Also, once you carry on running with a low level injury, the small changes in movement you are likely to make to 'nurse' the injury's site will, multiplied by the thousands of strides you will take, be likely to trigger off compensatory problems elsewhere.

CHAPTER 8

NUTRITION AND HYDRATION

'There should be no conflict between eating for health and eating for performance. The sound basis for a successful sporting diet is one based on healthy eating principles and a balanced approach.' That is the official UK Athletics introduction to its nutrition module for coaches. It provides a further eighteen pages, which should cover nearly all that coaches or athletes really need to know for their events. At first glance it seems strange that such a bland overview can be consistent with the ever-increasing volume of books about sports nutrition.

But before we look any further at what foods (or 'nutritional strategies', as we now seem obliged to describe them) may help your running, let's use some élite coaches' and athletes' wisdom for context. England Athletics' National Coach Mentor for Endurance, himself an Olympic athlete with a Masters in Sports Science, advised coaches: 'A good square meal backed up with quality snacking, breakfast and lunch usually provide 99 per cent of what you need,' while omitting how the other 1 per cent might be acquired.

'I eat the same as my wife, only more of it,' said Olympic 10,000-metre medallist Brendan Foster in his autobiography, written at his peak in the late 1970s. The book doesn't enlighten us on Mrs Foster's meal plans.

Fellow Geordie Olympic medallist Charlie Spedding writes this in his book: 'I think a lot of newcomers were hoping they could be able to eat themselves into peak physical condition … there were various fad foods and supplements and I was often asked if this or that food would improve performance.' He does observe, tongue in cheek, that cottage cheese must be a particularly unhelpful choice as he only ever sees obese people eating it. As a pharmacist and a meticulous planner, there is no suspicion that Spedding had an unduly casual approach – he simply evaluated its relative importance. His track record – he is still the English record-holder at marathon with 2.08.33 – suggests his judgement was spot-on.

I have spent hundreds of hours in coaching seminars and conferences with some of the best in the endurance business and, almost without exception, the coaches' presentations and ideas will not have nutrition at their heart and yet, invariably, questions from the floor will focus on nutrition far more than the presenting coach would have planned. The more experienced the coaches and athletes in attendance, the more they will keep nutrition where it belongs – it underpins running improvement but it certainly doesn't deliver it. For that, we have to leave the kitchen table and head out for some running.

Put another way, if you train very sensibly but eat a far from optimum diet you should still run close to your full potential. But if you train very haphazardly while following a nutritionally perfect plan for a healthy sporting life, you won't perform well as a distance runner. Indeed, research for this book came up with the following table, and bear in mind that in each case the book is written by a proven high level coach or sports scientist.

Title	Total page number	Total pages on diet including hydration and electrolytes	Pages on carboloading diet	Pages describing overemphasis on diet	Net pages on diet
Tim Noakes – *Lore of Running*	7 50 *(sic)*	47	7	3	37
Pfitzinger and Douglas – *Advanced Marathoning*	210	16	4	1	11
AAA *Runners' Guide*	190	10	2	1	7
Bruce Tulloh – *Running at 40+*	190	10	1	1	8
Jack Daniels – *Running Formula*	270	0	0	0	0
Cliff Temple – Marathon, Cross *Country and Road Running*	190	12	6	1	5
Dionisio Alonso – *Spanish Marathon Techniques*	280	18	5	2	11
David Costill – *Scientific Approach to Distance Running*	130	9	4	0	5

An interesting scenario, in which out of some 2,200 pages of the most influential guidance on long-distance running, about 4 per cent is allocated to nutrition and hydration other than the specific carbohydrate needs of a marathon. The rationale here is not that the writers don't care about nutrition – far from it – but rather that their expertise is based on a holistic approach to training the people they coach and the most significant part of this whole is the running itself. Similarly, these coaches and authors will be aware of the importance of the mental aspect of running, and of course the intricate world of injury treatment, but the publications on these areas, just as with nutrition, are written by those who have made these aspects, rather than the coaching, their focus.

Scouring some other volumes aimed more at beginner runners, the typical proportion on nutrition and hydration is between 10 and 15 per cent.

That said, it's obviously sensible to ensure as far as possible that you are covering the nutritional bases for your training and racing.

The Basic Food Groups and Requirements

Carbohydrates, proteins and fats are the three macronutrients that provide energy in a form that is necessary for survival. Alcohol is the only other source of energy, though that is not essential for survival, but you will more often hear runners saying 'I really need a pint' than they will mention a craving for some whey protein. If you are aware of the key elements of the food groups and maintain a good balance in line with your own training habits, you should be fuelling yourself adequately for your running.

Carbohydrates are the macronutrient that we need in the largest amounts. Depending on your level of physical activity, about 50–65 per cent of your energy should come from carbohydrate. Carbohydrates are the body's main source of fuel.

- Carbohydrates are easily used by the body for energy.
- All the tissues and cells in our body can use glucose (which is the usable form of carbohydrate after digestion) for energy.
- Carbohydrates are needed for the central nervous system, the kidneys, the brain, the muscles (including the heart) to function properly.
- Carbohydrates can be stored in the muscles and liver and later used for energy.

Complex carbs usually form a larger part of most runners' intake.

- Carbohydrates are important in intestinal health and waste elimination.
- Carbohydrates are mainly found in starchy foods (like grain, rice and potatoes), fruits, milk and yogurt. Other foods like vegetables, beans, nuts, and seeds contain carbohydrates, but in lesser amounts.

Fibre refers to certain types of carbohydrate that our body cannot digest. These carbohydrates pass through the intestinal tract intact and help to move waste out of the body. Diets that are low in fibre have been shown to cause problems such as constipation and haemorrhoids and to increase the risk for certain types of cancers. Diets high in fibre have been shown to reduce risks for heart disease and obesity, and they help lower cholesterol. Foods high in fibre include fruits, vegetables and wholegrain products.

Depending on individual activity levels, between 10 and 30 per cent of calories should come from **protein**. Most British people get plenty of protein and easily meet this need by consuming a balanced diet. We need protein for:

- growth (especially important for children, teenagers and pregnant women)
- tissue repair

- immune function
- making essential hormones and enzymes
- energy when carbohydrate is not available
- preserving lean muscle mass

Protein is found in meats, poultry, fish, meat substitutes, cheese, milk, nuts, legumes, and in smaller quantities in starchy foods and vegetables.

When we eat these types of food, our body breaks down the protein that they contain into amino acids (the building blocks of proteins). Some amino acids are essential, which means that we need to get them from our diet, and others are non-essential because our body can make them. Protein that comes from animal sources contains all the essential amino acids that we need. Plant sources of protein, on the other hand, do not contain all essential amino acids.

Although **fats** have received a bad reputation for causing weight gain, some fat is essential for survival. Between about 10 and 20 per cent of calories should come from fat. We need this amount of fat for:

- normal growth and development
- energy (fat is the most concentrated source of energy)

Dairy options can provide part of a healthy diet for most runners.

- absorbing certain vitamins (like vitamins A, D, E, K)
- providing cushioning for the organs
- maintaining cell membranes
- providing taste, consistency and stability to foods

Fat is found in meat, poultry, nuts, milk products, butters and margarines, oils, lard, fish, grain products and salad dressings. There are three main types of fat: saturated fat, unsaturated fat and trans fat. Saturated fat (found in foods like meat, butter, lard and cream) and trans fat (found in baked goods, snack foods, fried foods and margarines) have been shown to increase the risk of heart disease. Replacing saturated and trans fat in your diet with unsaturated fat (found in foods like olive oil, avocados and nuts) has been shown to decrease the risk of developing heart disease.

Some Specifics for Long-Distance Runners

Post-Training Refuelling Window

When you exercise aerobically you are running down your glycogen (carbohydrate) supplies and breaking down muscle tissues (protein, simplistically). Therefore to restore your body to its pre-training state you need to ingest a suitable quantity of carbohydrate and protein. An enzyme which is released during exercise enables your body to have a heightened capacity to absorb carbs and protein in a 30-minute window after training. A ratio of about 1 gram of carbohydrate and of 0.25 grams of protein per kilogram of bodyweight is shown to be the optimum to kick-start this recovery process. For most people this equates to a snack of about 300 to (for heavier runners) 400 calories of carb and protein, taken either as solid or as a specific sports recovery drink.

There is evidence that a balance of whey and casein protein is the particular structure of amino acid that helps the recovery process. Whey is the 'fast' protein that quickly enters the system to enable further protein synthesis to rebuild the muscles, while casein is the 'slow' protein that raises the amino acid levels in the bloodstream to ensure this rebuilding is sustained. So, in addition to the ever-increasing range of bespoke supplements provided by the sports nutrition sector, look for foods such as bread, yoghurt, soft low-fat cheese, tea cakes or scones, with low-fat filling, to fuel this snack.

Iron

It is worth giving particular focus to this mineral because it is so essential to your running performance. It is very easy to have a low level of iron, which will affect your running quite noticeably but which won't necessarily be picked up in a standard GP's blood test. This test looks at what is needed for 'general health', which, for the vast majority, means a fairly sedentary lifestyle.

We need to distinguish between iron deficiency anaemia – fairly rare in endurance runners: less than 2 per cent of women and even rarer in males – and the much more prevalent early symptoms of non-anaemic iron deficiency, which occurs in about 25–45 per cent of female runners and about 5 per cent of males. While anaemia most definitely has a major adverse effect on endurance performance, the more prevalent deficiency is not so conclusively shown to adversely affect your running, although most tests suggest that this is the case.

The 2011 European Athletics Federation's Endurance Conference included a keynote presentation on the subject, as an indicator of its importance. Iron is essential for red blood cell formation and thus the transportation and utilization of oxygen, so is at the heart of endurance capacity for any sport. Women need almost twice as high a daily intake as men – 14.8 miligrams vs 8.7 milograms. The best options for iron in a normal diet include red meat, breakfast cereals, green leafy vegetables, dried fruits, pulses, nuts and seeds. What needs to be considered are habits which can restrict iron absorption, including tea and coffee drunk within one hour either side of eating iron, high fibre intakes and zinc or calcium supplements.

The indicator of your iron level is your ferritin count. Ferritin is a measure of your body's iron stores. Normal reference ferritin levels are 12–200 ng (nanograms)/ml for women and 13–300 ng/ml for men. Ferritin is not directly related to performance but, if your ferritin level falls, eventually your haemoglobin and performances will decline too. Low ferritin, therefore, can be viewed as an early warning sign.

Ballpark figures suggest that training and racing performances are usually affected when ferritin levels drop below 20 ng/ml, and that when those athletes increase their ferritin levels to above 25 ng/ml they experience a rapid turnaround in performance. Bear in mind that counts in the 20s and low 30s are very common in distance runners. This is often the level at which your GP will not show

concern about any impact on your general health but where as a runner you may be convinced that something is not firing on all cylinders.

Low iron intake can be a problem for vegetarians, and for those runners who eat red meat less than once per week. The typical high-carbohydrate, low-fat, low-cholesterol runner's diet often includes little or no red meat. Red meat contains heme iron, which is more easily absorbed than plant sources of iron.

Another factor which may tilt the balance for some runners is foot strike hemolysis. This is the breakdown of red blood cells when the foot hits the ground. While foot strike hemolysis is not a big problem for most runners, if you are larger than average or run high mileage on asphalt, it could be a factor.

A relatively small amount of iron is lost through sweat and urine, but if you are doing heavy training in hot, humid conditions, this iron loss may add up. More research is needed to determine the magnitude of this problem.

You can only confirm your suspicions, however, with a blood test. You should find out both your haemoglobin and serum ferritin levels. Normal haemoglobin concentration ranges from 14 to 18 grams per 100ml of blood for men, and 12 to 16 grams per 100ml

Plenty of fresh veg should be a mainstay.

of blood for women, but for an endurance athlete the lower end of normal should be extended by about 1 gram per 100ml, due to larger blood volume.

The following actions should in most cases prevent iron deficiency:

- Eating 3oz/90g of lean red meat or dark poultry a couple of times per week.
- No coffee or tea with meals (that is, within an hour before or after), because they reduce iron absorption.
- Eating or drinking vitamin C-rich foods with meals to increase iron absorption.

Although these recommendations may seem like very subtle diet changes, they can have a powerful effect on your iron levels. For example, you will absorb three times as much iron from your cereal and toast if you switch from coffee to orange juice with breakfast. You should consider taking iron supplements, in the form of ferrous sulphate, ferrous gluconate or ferrous fumarate, only if necessary after making the recommended dietary changes.

Bodyweight

This is a sensitive issue for some, but it's naïve to ignore the indisputable fact that quicker runners are relatively light in bodyweight. If we remember that our maximum aerobic capacity (VO_2 max) is a bodyweight-based measurement, then basic science indicates that if all our aerobic and cardiovascular traits stay the same but we use these traits to shift a lighter body mass, we will go faster for a given level of effort.

Anecdotally, the author has noted that many very swift endurance runners are just not foodie types. Meals are simply refuelling for them – they eat, they start to feel full, they stop eating. These are the kinds of people who often struggle to keep their weight up when they are in heavy training, and when they are injured or eventually stop serious running they stay virtually the same weight, although their shape and muscle tone may slacken slightly over time.

To lose 1 pound or approximately 0.5 kilos you need to use up some 3,500 kilocalories more than you take in. Your running training will use up, at a weight of 10 stone/63 kilos, about 100 kcals per mile. Broadly pro rata this amount if you are lighter or heavier and also note that as long as you are running mainly aerobically this figure won't vary significantly with the running pace. Of course, the quicker you go the more calories per minute you use; and indeed, walking a mile uses a very similar amount of energy.

The psychology around food is a highly complex issue and not for this book. Losing a small amount of weight won't revolutionize your results. A 1k/2lb weight loss will, all other things being equal, bring about a performance improvement of between 1 per cent and a maximum of 2 per cent. It's hard to be exact because usually all other things aren't equal. Typically, an endurance athlete losing weight will also be undergoing some sort of changes in training volume and/or training intensity and/or planning structure and/or motivation and mental focus. So if a lighter athlete is making huge progress, be aware that he or she is probably also improving some other performance factors to achieve this.

We can all make personal choices on how important the extra few seconds per mile are when set against a second portion of an absolutely corking Bakewell tart. The witty American running writer Hal Higdon describes how, after weeks of hard purposeful training and two days of carbohydrate depletion before a marathon, he is let loose on a large ice cream sundae as he starts the loading phase. He writes that if told that each spoonful added a minute to his marathon time, he would carry on fuelling until he hit the excess half-hour mark. For broad brush guidance on losing some weight to aid running performance, try to adhere to the following:

- Do make it gradual – 1kg/2lb per fortnight maximum.
- Do ensure you stay hydrated and don't 'manipulate' weight loss through dehydration.
- Don't cut back on your basic complex carbohydrate or protein needs, or eliminate fat from your diet. You need all these to ensure some sort of quality for your training and recovery, let alone the daily business of normal life. Instead, cut back

General health guidelines for alcohol are suitable for most runners.

on the empty calories of refined carbohydrates, saturated fats and alcohol. Alcohol can be doubly villainous in that it provides 'useless' calories and also tends to reduce the willpower to resist other foods.

Caffeine

There is increasingly robust information that an intake of caffeine can boost long-distance performance because it has the effect of enabling the use of fatty acids as an energy source. Tests in 2008 on some non-élite runners showed that, all other things being equal, a supplement of 5mg of caffeine per kilogram of bodyweight led to about a 1.5 per cent increase in performance. That is about 40–50 seconds in a 10k race. Based on the caffeine content of typical drinks, this converts very roughly to about 1–1.5 litres of Coca Cola, 1 litre of Red Bull or comparable drink, about three to four 250-millilitre cups of brewed coffee or about five cups of instant coffee. There is now also a range of gels, bars and capsules which provide suitable levels of caffeine boost. The time frame for ingesting this caffeine is about 30–75 minutes before the event starts. That's quite a lot of coffee or cola to drink in a short time frame and different individuals will have different responses to this sort of regime. It is definitely not advisable to try this for the first time before a big target race, but instead to test it out in a couple of long training runs to check your overall response to the supplementation.

The side effects of excess caffeine on a regular basis are well known to many people with no involvement in running. They can include anxiety, dizziness, restlessness and insomnia – all related to the 'buzz' that caffeine gives to the nervous system – so in this case more is definitely not better. You should not take the above-mentioned quantities of caffeine on a continuous basis, because in addition to the adverse health effects you will minimize the performance boost as your body becomes accustomed to having excess caffeine as its normal state.

Omega 3

These are a type of polyunsaturated fat found naturally in fish oils, which have long been considered to have a range of health benefits both mental and physical. Recent studies at the University of California showed that Omega 3 fatty acids can increase the efficiency of the cardiovascular system, which is clearly something that endurance runners are looking to experience. The results broadly correlated with a 2008 study in Australia on highly trained cyclists. The tests used fish oil supplements (with olive oil or sunflower oil provided to the control group) and showed that there is a link between higher levels of the relevant fatty acids provided in fish oil and cardiovascular efficiency. In a separate test in Australia, fish oils were shown to reduce body fat in people exercising regularly, the theory being that the fish oils help the mitochondria (the 'energy factories' within cells) to convert fatty acids into energy. Beside the 'cosmetic' aspect of reduced body fat, this may also be relevant to endurance performance where the oxidization of fatty acids in longer races is known to be a less efficient system than using glycogen (derived from carbohydrate) as the main energy source. Mackerel, salmon, herrings, sardines and pilchards are the most Omega 3-rich foods.

IF YOU CAN'T BEET 'EM…

Beetroot juice seems to 'work' in terms of improving endurance, is easily available, is natural, has no known long-term adverse effects on health, and is therefore legal within all competition rules. In brief, studies at the University of Exeter in 2009 led by Professor Andy Jones, who just happens to be the lead physiologist employed by UK Athletics to work with élite endurance runners, showed that in controlled experiments people could cycle up to 16 per cent longer with a daily half-litre of beetroot juice, and that on a test at high intensity to exhaustion a 2 per cent improvement was noted, on average. Professor Jones stated his 'amazement' at the results, believed to be related to the high nitrate levels in beetroot forming nitric oxide and requiring less oxygen to be taken in to maintain a given level of aerobic effort. He made the caveat that the tests were done using cycling rather than running and the subjects were not élite athletes. For an élite athlete 2 per cent is a big gain, especially if it is risk-free, guaranteed and can be gained in such a simple process as a pint of vegetable juice.

It would be very hard, however, for a distance runner making a 2 per cent improvement in real competition performance (as opposed to a lab test) to isolate the progression to just one factor such as beetroot juice. That said, in autumn 2011 two Canadian élite marathoners both ran notable PBs in Toronto, securing selection for the 2012 Olympics. One took a pint (half a litre) of beetroot juice with his pre-race meal, the other took the same amount about two days before the race (having had stomach problems with drinking it too close to the race time).

There is no evidence that longer term beetroot juice intake produces any further aerobic gains so, thankfully, runners need not contemplate a lifetime of discharging dark purple urine. At the time of writing, it is a case of 'watch this space' or, more specifically, check out www.beet-it.com, which is probably the first time a Suffolk vegetable farm has been so closely linked to high performance sports science.

CHAPTER 9

VETERAN RUNNERS

Go to almost any long-distance road race outside national élite competition and the first thing you may notice is the large number of runners who are slightly past their first flush of youth. In fact it may be difficult to pick out any runners in their early or mid-20s, their physical prime.

Although many veterans or masters competitions include a 35 to 39-year-old age group, this chapter will consider veterans running as starting at 40. Long-distance runners are very much at the height of their endurance prowess at age 35, which they can hold for a further two or three years, so age 40 is when some of the 'vets only' factors start to come into play.

Depending on a whole host of factors, these new runners often become hooked and are as much a part of the running community as the high performers at county and regional level. Indeed in some cases these *arrivistes* actually become the leading county and regional runners if they have been blessed with good genes and follow a high performance training plan for some years.

The fastest world performances in the various age categories over 40 are in their way as mind-blowing as the world records in the standard senior ranks.

In many ways, therefore, the best practice guidelines for senior runners can be and are applicable to veteran runners. However, there are various factors that runners over 40 need to consider, which younger runners may be able to put on the back burner for some years.

Long May You Run

In researching his book on veteran runners, Bruce Tulloh's survey of over 200 40-pluses found 'as many different patterns as there are individuals', which chimes neatly with my own view that 'each athlete is an experiment of one'.

We've all seen those questionnaires asking why we run, with reasons from 'wanting to compete for Great Britain' to ' being able to eat plenty of cake without turning into Michelin man', and covering factors such as health and fitness, desire to test one's limits, bringing structure and contrast to busy but often sedentary lifestyles, and social networks.

Most of these factors will apply to most runners but the relative priority will vary immensely. The Olympic runner won't run 120 miles a week to make more friends or ensure her jeans fit well, but she'll be aware that these are positive results from her running life. The man trying to beat 45 minutes for a 10k won't relocate to an Ethiopian hillside to achieve this, but he might moderate his Saturday night beer and curry intake. Experienced runners who face the inevitable fact that as they get past their late 30s and particularly into their mid- to late 40s their race times will be heading south, may change their running goals and priorities, maybe in ways they wouldn't have expected in earlier years.

However, aside from various inspiring case histories, there are trends – look at the world age category records in the tables below.

Men's 10,000m track – age group	Mark	Name	Country	Age
M 40	28:30.88	Martti Vainio	FIN	40
M 45	30:02.56	Antonio Villanueva	MEX	45
M50	30:55.16	Peter De Vocht	BEL	50
M 55	32:27.7	Michael F. Hager	GBR	55
M 60	34:14.88	Luciano Acquarone	ITA	60
M 65	34:42.2	Derek Turnbull	NZL	65
M 70	38:04.13	Ed Whitlock	CAN	70
M 75	39:25.16	Ed Whitlock	CAN	75

Women's 10,000m track – age group	Mark	Name	Country	Age
W 40	31:40.97	Alla Zhilyayeva	RUS	40
W 45	32:34.06	Evy Palm	SWE	46
W 50	35:41.90	Gitte Karlsjöj	DEN	50
W 55	37:09.4	Sandra Branney	GBR	55
W 60	39:04.23	Bernadine Portenski	NZL	60
W 65	42:07.1	Theresia Baird	AUS	65
W 70	47:22.51	Melitta Czerwenka-Nagel	GER	70
W 75	50:00.93	Melitta Czerwenka-Nagel	GER	70

Once you've finished marvelling at how people of these ages can run so fast, you will notice that invariably these global marks are set by athletes in the first year or two of the relevant five-year age bands. Statistically inclined readers can also do the maths to monitor the rate of decline. By and large it is in the region of 2 to 4 seconds per mile per year.

In terms of what you as a 40-plus might achieve, see if all or most of the following apply and you might still have some latent PBs in the tank:

- less than five years of any regular running
- less than two years of 'proper' structured and challenging running training

- carrying a few extra kilos of weight
- never really focused on what you might achieve as a runner beyond general aerobic fitness
- poor nutritional and alcohol habits
- never spent quality time on any non-running training elements relating to strength/strength endurance, flexibility, technique and running form.

Clearly we can't quantify the performance gains related to any of the above, but in my view they are listed in order of relative significance. To illustrate this, one can find national level or even international runners with rather sketchy credentials on the two final factors, but you will be unlikely to unearth a runner of that level who hasn't ticked the first two boxes.

Age Grading: Measuring Up

Most veteran readers will be aware of the age-grading tables, a simple mathematical calculation that uses the world age best for each single age in each event, so that every performance is shown as a percentage of the world's best. So a 46-year-old man doing a 22-minute 5k can compare his result to, for example, a 41-year-old woman doing 24 minutes in the same race. It's not unusual for the top age-graded performance at an event to be by someone who doesn't feature at the very front of the race. For runners who have reached an age and stage where their absolute times are slowing down, maintaining or improving their age-graded rating can be a highly motivating factor. Generally, those who came to the sport later in life seem to be more focused on this benchmarking of performance, whereas the traditional harrier types who have come through the ranks as youngsters tend to be less driven by the stats, even though they may be running fairly swiftly.

Vets Medical Factors

'Focus areas' for veterans have been highlighted by physical therapist Gerard Hartmann, who has highly rated medical credentials in endurance sport. As a key physiotherapy back-up provider to the likes of Paula Radcliffe, World Champion Sonia O'Sullivan, and Olympic 1500m Champion Noah Ngeny of Kenya, amongst many other big hitters, he is considered in the endurance running world to have 'magic hands' because of the precision of his diagnoses and treatments. His most notable veteran link was with Irish legend Eamonn Coghlan, who ran a 3.58-mile aged 41, a staggering achievement at that age.

He precedes the specifics by suggesting that 'stress is the most silent killer. Everyone has a different tolerance to stress and it is very much individually registered'. This isn't the forum to look in detail at the huge diversity of people's lifestyles, but as a general practical point for runners he says, 'Many athletes squeeze their training into hectic workdays – I question the wisdom of this.' Of course, how you balance this if your pursuit of endurance prowess is unavoidably and inextricably bound up with factors like a full-time job, parenting of young children, travelling to and from work, and some sort of family and social network where not everyone builds their plans around your PB-hunting, is up to each individual.

He does, however, focus on veteran runners maintaining a lower bodyweight, normally linked to a lower percentage of body fat, for all the usual reasons related to performance, recovery, injury prevention and – linked to an ample intake of anti-oxidants – a healthy immune system.

Further advice:

- Muscle strength and muscle mass fall between about 30 per cent and 50 per cent between the ages of 30 and 70.

The strength and conditioning elements described in this book are therefore highly relevant to veterans – if anything they are even more fundamental, because as the ageing joints in the knees, hips and ankles weaken, they are ever more vulnerable to injury if the major and core muscle groups are not taking their optimum share of the impact of running.

- Flexibility decreases as the body's collagen and elasticin content changes in composition. Hartmann unequivocally suggests 'at least 10 minutes per day' of stretching.
- This is linked to his recommendation to keep some faster paced running as a regular training element. The preparation for and execution of this pace will involve dynamic stretching to maintain or at least constrain the decreasing range of movement which nature is causing.
- Also linked to flexibility and elasticity are running drills which break down the running movement into key elements and look at maximizing the quality of these. These include:
  - Fast feet , moving as if you are stepping on hot coals, so minimizing ground contact.
  - High knees, done as a walk-through with one foot on the ground at all times, bringing the knee up through to waist level, keeping the trunk held high and erect.
  - Once the high knees drill is done efficiently, bring in an exaggerated arm action, so that as the thigh is raised the opposite hand is brought up to the forehead, ensuring it doesn't cross the body.

Typically, do each drill for about 10 seconds, about three times. This duration is about the right amount time to get into and repeat the movement to whatever is your best level, stopping before fatigue creeps in and compromises the quality of movement and also probably your concentration.

Joint Problems

This section is about osteoarthritis – for ageing runners perhaps the most frequent injury problem that is veteran-specific.

We've all had the naysayers telling us how 'all that wear and tear on the legs' must be damaging in the long term, and in particular the threat of osteoarthritis. Clearly in a degenerative condition that affects a significant number of people in middle and older age, there are going to be numerous runners who also suffer from it; this is just simple statistics and probability.

Fortunately there is some robust research, and maybe the most informative is the data used by Arthritis Research and Therapy obtained from the Fifty Plus Runners Association in the USA. Over a fourteen-year timescale it compared runners as they progressed through their 50s and 60s, with a control group of non-runners. The runners averaged 26 miles per week training, regular but not 'high mileage' as such. They experienced about 25 per cent less musculoskeletal pain than the non-runners. It's notable that this is a perception by the runners, not a medical diagnosis, but for practical purposes it is sensible to know how we will feel as we continue running in our later years. The Arthritis Council has stated directly: 'The stronger the muscles and tissues around your joints, the better they will be able to support and protect those joints. If you don't exercise, your muscles become smaller and weaker.'

The caveat to this is when a runner has had an injury around a joint and the nature of the healing process – combined with a return to running which has maybe continued to 'stretch the envelope' more than is ideal, and well in excess of those 26 miles per week mentioned above – has left a structural weakness. Over time this does indeed leave the area vulnerable to osteoarthritis. Research indicates that 75 per cent of sportspeople with the disease experience it on a site where there has been a previous injury to the affected joint that has adversely affected the quantity or strength of the cartilage. In the large majority of runners this will be the knee.

Supplements for Osteoarthritis

Collagen hydrolysate supplements are rich in amino acids, which have a key role in synthesizing collagen, a major component of joint cartilage. So the simple theory is that rebuilding and/or strengthening existing cartilage can ease the symptoms of arthritis. Arthritis Research UK's latest position on this is that relevant trials 'are scarce and yielded mixed results'. It rates its effectiveness as 2 out of 5. So it's not a miracle cure for all and the tests aren't runner-specific. However, if you are one of those runners for whom the '2 out of 5' score has a practical benefit that enables you to run with less discomfort, it's maybe worth using.

Chondroitin sulphate exists naturally in the body and is thought to give cartilage elasticity and to slow its breakdown. In supplement form it is often taken alongside glucosamine to relieve the symptoms of osteoarthritis. There is no proof that it reverses cartilage loss, but some studies suggest it helps stop joint degeneration. Chondroitin is a slow-acting supplement, so don't expect to see any improvement for at least two months. It doesn't help everyone – if you have severe cartilage loss you probably won't get any benefit. There do not appear to be any serious side effects, but minor ones include occasional nausea and indigestion. It could increase your chances of bleeding if you are taking any blood-thinning drugs. The long-term effects of taking chondroitin are not known.

Depending on the product and the level of bulk buying you will commit to, supplements based on the compounds above typically cost about £25 for a month's supply.

Each runner should bear in mind that the rate at which the problem may worsen will vary between individuals. But a more universal factor is that on each long run the shock absorption traits of the joints are weakened in the latter miles of a longer run, which may lead some affected runners to focus their training and racing on 5ks, 10ks and maybe half marathons, with a view to 'running longevity'. Bear in mind that the above-mentioned survey average of 26 miles per week would probably not have included many very long runs.

Recovery and Training Structures

One trend that very few ageing runners will be able to ignore is that the time needed to recover between hard sessions, and indeed between any training sessions, becomes longer. We need to respect this and work out constructive ways to manage it without it affecting performance more than is necessary. Even runners in their mid- to late 30s performing at the very highest level acknowledge that they have to revise some of their training habits from ten years earlier.

Certainly the practice of doing harder efforts on alternate days three times per week, which is hard to sustain at any age, becomes very hard to manage successfully in the veteran age groups, particularly if there is a purposeful long run to be done at the weekend.

Tim Noakes's authoritative book *The Lore of Running* even goes so far as to advise veteran runners to look at a planned programme of alternate days running and cross-training (cycling, in the examples he mentions), with a couple of case histories of how, at a high level, performances at 10k seemed to thrive off this balance. One case was an ex-Olympic runner with a 28.30 PB who was nudging 32 minutes in his mid-40s. Great running, undoubtedly, but he'd needed to deal physically and mentally with a drop-off rate of some 35 seconds per mile over about fifteen years, which is within the typical range of decline mentioned earlier. The volume and duration of cycling mentioned was substantial, so this isn't a cop-out but an alternative means to strong performance. His recommendations, however, did not cover:

- what sort of age these concessions to the ageing process should start, so 39¾-year-olds running six days a week shouldn't have to cut their mileage in half as soon as they hit 40;
- the balance of harder sessions and recovery sessions between running and cross-training.

There are no hard and fast rules on the frequency of sessions but some of the following should be borne in mind:

- If you aren't already doing so, look at training in terms of what you want to cover in a 14- or 28-day period rather than a brief 7-day weekly cycle.
- Where lifestyle commitments allow, don't be bound to rituals on certain days of the week. It's often hard to find time and energy for very long runs on days within a Monday to Friday working pattern, but with the increasing options of family-friendly working life there may be flexibility. Also, don't feel obliged to turn up at the club or group Tuesday reps session just because it's there and it's Tuesday. When planning your training it may be enlightening to just number the days 1 to 14 or 1 to 28 rather than feel constrained by what a given day usually entails. As an extreme case of how we can get stuck in our ways, I was once asked by a runner if there was some biological or biorhythmic reason why the body couldn't train hard on a Friday as all the training schedules she'd seen in magazines and websites always showed Friday as a rest day.

- Think about maybe four harder efforts per 14 days or five harder efforts per 21 days and accept that as you get older you will probably have to gradually increase the number of recovery/easy days in between the harder efforts.
- But do still push the harder efforts just as hard as you can, as you did when you were younger. The race distances aren't shortened to reflect your added years, and 100 per cent effort is 100 per cent effort at any age, though the speed at which you cover the ground at 100 per cent effort may reduce.
- Some of the advice in Chapter 4 about aerobic cross-training may therefore become more relevant as you age. The balancing act between preparing specifically to do long-distance road races and protecting your joints from the repeated impact of long-distance road-running will evolve over time. You can't prepare thoroughly and exclusively by cross-training, but you may think about doing some of the steady state training as non-running, interspersed between the harder efforts done on the run. The cardiovascular, aerobic and fat-burning effects will be very similar for a given level of intensity but you would avoid the exponential wear and tear on your joints that the final stages of a long training run would bring.

Cross-Training Dominant

M	40min easy run including 7 or 8 × 20sec strides
T	X-trainer – w/up then alternate weekly sessions of e.g. 10 × 3min at 5k effort with 60sec 'jog' or 5 × 6min at 10k effort with 60sec 'jog'
W	50min easy run
T	55/60min easy steady run
F	X-trainer – around threshold effort, for example simulation of 'out and back' session of 25min at notional half marathon effort followed by 20min at 10k to 10-mile race pace
S	Rest
S	Elliptical X-trainer – 2hr, first hour to 70 easy/comfortable, last 50/60min at notional marathon effort
Total aerobic volume	20 miles easy to steady running, plus three harder cross-training sessions

Running Dominant

M	55min easy X-trainer
T	Running – interval session alternating weeks of e.g. 6 or 7 × 4.5min at c. 5k pace with 2min jog recovery with 11 or 12 × 2min reps at c. 3k pace with 60sec recovery
W	50min easy run
T	60min steady pace run
F	Harder running session – alternate weeks of w/up then 45/50min sustained running, progressing from notional marathon pace to about 10-mile race pace, alternate with long reps at about 10-mile race pace e.g. 4 × 10 or 11min with 2min jog or 5 × 8 or 9min with 90sec jog
S	Rest
S	1hr 45 to 1hr 50 run, easy start, last 30min at notional marathon effort
Total aerobic volume	47 miles running, including two harder sessions plus one easy X-train session

Integration of Cross-Training

Below are two typical, simple schedules followed by a 45-year-old man who was running the occasional 10k in 38 to 38.30 – he had a PB of 33.00 set twenty years earlier when he had regularly run around 80 to 90 miles per week and was about 5kg lighter. The obvious major difference is the running volume. The fact that after adhering to both schedules for some months the running performance was very similar is consistent with Noakes's comments.

The other more subtle difference is that the elliptical gives a slightly less intense challenge than running, so that repetitions that could be run at something between 1500m and 3–5k pace tended to be more like 5–10k effort on the cross-trainer. So the intense sessions on the elliptical tend to go for slightly longer reps, slightly less recovery and slightly more total duration of reps than running sessions would entail. The occasional short rep session on the cross-trainer would be something like thirty-two to thirty-five reps of 35 to 40 seconds done at about 3k effort (by perceived rate of effort) on a 60-second cycle – thus giving a recovery of 20 or 25 seconds. It's slightly less gruelling on the cross-trainer, because if done as a running session the aim would be to pace it at very close to your speed at VO_2 max – or vVO_2 max, to represent 'velocity' – whereas on an elliptical it's hard to make the arm and leg movement quick enough to achieve this intensity. It may suit whirling dervishes, though.

In another upbeat case history, I coached for some years a mid-40s runner with a keen interest in canoeing. During this period the athlete never ran more than four times a week, and usually three times. He combined this with, for most of the year, one or two structured and tough canoe sessions and one strength/strength endurance session each week. During this period, between age 43 and age 46, having already had three years of running training in the bank, his half marathon time improved by 4 minutes and his 10k time also improved significantly, at an age when it is usually hard for seasoned runners to prevent some slippage. And this on top of the fact that muscular endurance in canoeing has different priorities compared to running – a look at elite canoeists' upper bodies illustrates this. However, to show how, cardiovascularly, endurance coaches are singing from a similar hymn sheet in various sports, there was one bittersweet day when the athlete did a running session of twenty-five reps of 200 metres in the morning, then pitched up at the canoe club in the evening where the club session was, of course, twenty-four reps of 200 metres.

CHAPTER 10

TECHNOLOGY

Physiological Testing

With technology now so integrated into sport at all levels and many people curious to see how they measure up physiologically in what is technically a fairly simple sport, a growing number of runners are having occasional tests at either university sports performance labs or private companies operating the same sorts of services. In summary, they offer a protocol that will, on a given day, assess your VO_2 max, your lactate threshold, your lactate turnpoint (or anaerobic threshold) and your running economy. The report will also provide some generic training recommendations based on your results. A few things to bear in mind if you wish to tap into this service:

- The test will take you to your maximum aerobic capacity and then beyond, so it will be very intense although not that long in duration.
- You should not train beyond very easy effort for two days previously so that you are fresh and unfatigued for the test and can perform to your maximum.
- An experienced coach should be able to assess where your relative strengths and weaknesses are by looking at your best times over a range of endurance distances and assessing how your running and any other aerobic training have evolved over the months and years.
- Remember that the VO_2 max is bodyweight-related; whatever scientific exper-

tise you tap into, extra bodyweight will be a significant factor. Or, as one wag posted on a running forum: 'A miracle, all I did was lose some weight and my VO_2 max went up.'
- A one-off test is of relatively modest value, because your PBs will probably tell the story of how your physiology is suited to running performance, and there is always a margin of error of up to 10 per cent built into a one-off test. That's a big margin if you apply that percentage to performance. If you are a 45-minute 10k runner you don't want a set of data that is more akin to a 41-minute or 49-minute runner. I stress this point because, almost without exception, everyone I coach who has at some point had this battery of tests done as a one-off, has had a VO_2 max that is typically in line with significantly quicker performances than they have achieved (about 5–8 per cent in most cases). As one subject, himself an Assistant Professor in Neuroscience as well as a nippy 15-minute 5k runner, commented, 'We can't all have the world's worst running economy.'
- Note that the data will, typically, be gathered by increasing the pace in increments of 1 kilometre per hour, or maybe 0.5 kilometres per hour, and the paces for aerobic threshold, lactate turnpoint and vVO_2 max extrapolated from these. You might therefore not actually do any running at the exact pace at which the lactate turn-

point is reached. Instead, the turnpoint will be shown by 'joining the dots' of increasing pace vs increased blood lactate. Consequently, in training, don't think there is an exact pace to be hit to test the turnpoint, and that anything either side of this is lacking in precision. To illustrate this, when Alberto Salazar was presenting at a UK Athletics conference in 2011, he mentioned that Mo Farah, when working at this sort of effort, might do something like 5 × 1 mile/1600 meters at 4 minutes 20 seconds, with a short recovery (that's about his 10,000m race pace), or up to 45 or 50 minutes at around 4 minutes 45 to 4 minutes 50 seconds, or some variation between these two. Clearly this pace range is too slow to test the top end of Farah's VO_2 max, and slightly too fast to be his aerobic threshold/marathon pace, but Salazar was confident that playing around with these paces would still be addressing the lactate challenge.

- That caveat aside, if you do go for a series of tests over time, the typical evolution will be the following: your running economy will show the greatest longer term rate of progress; your turnpoint will have the next most noticeable trend of improvement; while your VO_2 max (assuming stable weight over the period) will show the most modest level of progression.

New Shoe Advances

Before you become frazzled searching for the perfect shoe, it's worth noting that all the major shoe companies have a range of shoes to cover all bases: neutral, pronator, supinator, road racer, road trainer, off-road and so on, and that they all bring out a new model of each model almost every year. One wonders how much shoe technology changes on an annual basis, and indeed it would be strange if such technological progression occurred on such a neat linear calendar basis – which is why I claim far from encyclopaedic knowledge on the multitude of options.

It's also noticeable that while all the big brands have embraced the barefoot and minimalist options as part of their range, they have also carried on making all their traditional models. Shoe companies are starting to focus more on how the shoes are shaped, in the hope of providing better support and stability for a more natural feel. Environmental factors are also now taken into account: some manufacturing changes may be flagged up by a brand but without making significant differences to performance or comfort. And no one has yet claimed that a particular colour of shoe enables faster performance…

Some of the old truisms hold good. Once you have found a model and brand that suits you, stick with it as far as that model stays in production. It's worth having a gait and stride analysis provided by many stores as part of the sales service. Typically the person who advises you on this will be a runner with some knowledge of what to observe and what the implications are. But don't expect everyone who works in a running store to be at the cutting edge of biomechanics.

One experienced retail manager, referring to the class of 2013 in terms of performance aspects and environmental factors, said, 'You're seeing a lot of lower heel-to-toe differential, so heel heights in the shoe are coming down in order to allow more midfoot stride. A lot of people find it easier to land midfoot and use your arch to absorb shock. Cushioning technology in shoes is also seeing a dramatic change for the first time in more than forty years. Previously, shoes were made with ethylene vinyl acetate, known as EVA, a foam material that would take up to 1,000 years to biodegrade. Traditionally, this material takes about 1,000 years to biodegrade in landfill. BioMoGo is a type of EVA that biodegrades fifty times faster, so it will biodegrade in twenty years.'

With that in mind, here are some snippets on some of the new technology that has hit the shelves in 2013/14:

'Boost' makes use of thermoplastic polyurethane, which has been used in footwear before, but now it's taken and used in pellet form and made into a consistent shoe with great rebound. It provides a slightly smoother running experience than foam shoes because foam shoes actually break down relatively quickly.

The 'PureCadence' came out of the barefoot movement. It's a less extreme version, whereby instead of squeezing the foot, the foot is spread out and moves more naturally. It changes the way the heel contacts the ground by moving the heel forward and creating a more natural anatomic shape.

A rival company has put in flex grooves, which actually mimic the joints of your foot. Previously they were trying to mechanically dissipate shock; now the focus is on the anatomical construction of your foot so that the shoe can respond a lot more easily to the natural motion of your body – in theory a more individually adapted shoe. Another advance in shoe technology is chips installed in the shoe to tell the runner the distance covered and the relevant speed. Runners can look at the information about their run through an app on their iPhone or iPod.

Another innovative design is named after the town which hosts the University of Central Lancashire, where the shoe was designed. It is the brainchild of a Yorkshire-based mattress company and a biomechanics professor, who hope their product will significantly reduce the risk of injury from running. Their model uses the same technology as a pocket-sprung mattress, with lightweight micro springs meaning that significantly more shock and pressure can be absorbed, as well as an increased uplift as you push back off the ground.

Research leader Professor Jim Richards teamed up with a mattress company to use a version of one of their high-end pocket springs, called the 'e Spring', into the sole of a trainer. Professor Richards said: 'Despite the advances in running shoe technology, there is still the huge problem of injury. What's different about our shoe is the spring technology combined with the damper. If you had a car suspension with just a damper and no spring in it then you'd have a very bumpy ride. Therefore, having a shoe that incorporates both provides a much improved shock absorbing system. We can also tweak the arrangement for each individual runner, which is particularly important because everyone has a different running style and physiology, which affects their risk of different types of injury.'

At the time of writing the shoes had been 'revealed' to the public at The Royal Society Summer Science Exhibition but were not yet available on a retail basis.

Heart Rate Monitors

Heart rate monitors are not unlike treadmills in terms of runners' enthusiasm for them. There are those who won't go near them, and others who won't go running without them, and all shades of engagement across the range. By and large, the majority of high performance coaches and athletes see the technology as crucial to their training programmes. 'Heart-rate monitors are an essential part of race success,' says Marcus O'Sullivan, head of Villanova University's highly successful track programme and a former World Indoor Champion himself. 'It's very hard for me to coach an athlete who won't wear one.'

Former UK marathon star Jon Brown, twice fourth in the Olympics and now a sought-after coach in the New Zealand élite triathlon world, similarly suggested that all serious runners should learn to regularly use a monitor simply 'to make the hard runs hard and the easy runs easy'. A relevant quote on heart rate comes from Guillermo Ferrero, coach to Spanish 10,000 metres record-holder Fabian Roncero, who said, 'Heart rate is just an indicator of the state; lactate level is the state itself.'

However, if one of the attractions of running is its simplicity away from the hassles and restrictions of your daily life, you may be averse to charting your training against a precise set of data, and instead prefer to rely on perceived effort and pace judgement, particularly if you have some experience of racing and training at different paces. And of course, if some of the greatest runners in the world can get by without using HRM in most of their training, it can't be an absolute essential. I have coached for some years a national level athlete (just over 8 minutes for 3,000 metres) and he is a scientist by education, clocking up a biochemistry degree at Oxford University as well as being a voracious student of the sport. He has not yet monitored his training by HRM, but uses various other tools to gauge effort, performance and, importantly, recovery.

If you are going to use one with any robustness, do check your resting heart rate and your maximum rate – the latter will require you to do a very hard session to an exhausted anaerobic state. This should be within three or so beats of your maximum. Bear in mind that your maximum is not something you can train to improve, indeed it will gradually decline with age (on average about one beat per minute per year). The improvement is of course based around your improved efficiency (and specifically running pace)

at sub-maximal levels of maximum heart rate.

Also be aware that resting heart rates have a genetic element. Whilst a fit endurance athlete, in any sport, will have a resting heart rate (RHR) very much lower than the average sedentary person's 70–80, the range of lower RHR is not that closely correlated to running performance. Some fantastic runners, therefore, may be in the mid- to high 40s, while some much more humble club runners may clock in at slightly under 40.

Now, to make the equipment ever more usable and accessible, companies are offering devices that are sleeker and packed with more features. At the top end of the sales stats, and with a suitably high profile in the running world, is Garmin's Forerunner 405, which has vaulted the company past Polar in the market in distance and heart-rate tracking watches. 'The heart-rate straps work better, the displays are easy to read, and there's more useful information,' says Greg McMillan, an exercise physiologist and well respected coach of élite, club and recreational runners. 'Garmin and other companies are trying to move from simply delivering information to having the device tell you what to do.'

A detailed set of case studies carried out in the USA by a very well-known running magazine used a range of varied level runners, both in performance and experience. It produced some excellently quotable quotes, but in parts it seemed to work on the assumption that some runners had particularly short supplies of intelligence and common sense, and no access to either the internet or indeed their own magazine to fill in some of these gaps.

So, there is one runner who, after a few months of starting the sport from scratch, downloaded the data after an easy-paced 6k run and was baffled by what the stats indicated. He logged a 173 heartbeats-per-minute average, which the watch says is

96 per cent of his maximum. That's the effort of a highly trained athlete in the painful final laps of a 5K. Legendary USA coach, author and exercise physiologist Dr Jack Daniels, put these numbers in perspective. He advised that most fitness watches calculate maximum heart rate based on a mathematical formula. 'Those age-based formulae have a wide standard deviation, and some runners are outliers.'

Daniels has tested hundreds of athletes and found so many outliers that he now ignores the equations. For instance, a 30-year-old Olympian once showed a maximum of 148 beats, putting him at 72 years of age according to the watch's formula. Maximum heart rate is merely a function of how much blood the ventricles pump with each contraction, and, as with resting heart rate mentioned above, has an element of genetics in the numbers. The runner in question described the watch's supposed easy effort band as 'basically the zone I use when making a sandwich'. Eagle-eyed readers will note that sandwich-making has yet to appear on any of the more respected lists for cross-training.

Within the study, a 2:19 marathoner and running coach highlighted that heart-rate monitors are especially good for providing structure for raw beginners. 'First-time runners are like little kids. They sprint 200 yards down the street and collapse. It feels hard, they get discouraged, and they never want to do it again.'

Another studied runner aimed to take her running to a higher level, but apparently had no idea how to pace herself or mix hard runs with recovery jogs. (Perhaps she lives in a place where books and internet haven't yet arrived.) The watch she experimented with provided a guideline plan, suggesting workouts in three zones – light, moderate and hard. It assigned a quota of 5.5 total hours of weekly exercise, with the majority in the easy zone. The light workout pace was a revelation;

it was the speed she usually jogged alongside her ageing dog. 'Now that I'm not running full steam at every workout, I have more energy,' she says.

On some days, the watch flashed messages, such as, 'You have not recovered from last week, it was too hard.' Other times it prompted, 'You did a good job. Keep it up!' So the runner started to think of it as 'an adult Tamagotchi, needing constant attention or it'll die'. She found that her running was taking on another dimension. 'This is the first time it goes beyond thinking about the size of my ass. I'm running because I like seeing the progress.' Runners can form their own assessment of where a flashing watch's messages fit into their own motivational hierarchy.

Just as the watch guides her on when to take it easy, it shows her how to run hard. Once she was physically ready, she ran mile efforts to fill the 'hard' requirements on the watch. She ran three repeats of 1 mile, keeping her heart between 80 and 90 per cent of maximum with a 2-minute rest. At the end of the week, she earned an 'Excellent!' from the watch's rewards and recognition system. This may or may not be a higher commendation than an excellent with no exclamation mark.

While a dinky wristwatch assessing your general fitness is strange, one that tells your future is even stranger. Polar claims that its fitness test can predict VO_2 max, the upper limit of an athlete's oxygen intake and an important indicator of innate endurance talent in runners. The study tasked the chair of the kinesiology department at the University of Massachusetts with measuring the runner's VO_2 max during a treadmill test to find out if it matched the watch's calculations. The test gave a VO_2 max of 51.2, a high number for a runner of the woman's age. The watch was right; in fact its calculations had slightly shortchanged her. 'I guess

I have more potential than I thought,' she reflected, and indeed this prompted her to take her running even more seriously in the ensuing months.

Greg McMillan sees these devices as a means to uncover your own best athlete within. He summarizes: 'These tools can help you learn from your body, but you have to use your own brain. The idea is to find what works for you. That has to be an experiment of one.'

Calories Burned on the Run

This section is included more for general interest than because in my view it is a particularly useful detail for improving performance. It is no more nor less important than the content of Chapter 4 on nutrition indicates. Given the array of technology now available and its huge prominence in the food, health and leisure industries, we should be able to reliably monitor how many calories a runner burns by running at a given running pace, or for a given running distance.

But things aren't always so simple. A tester ran an 8-minute mile pace on a treadmill for 40 minutes and tracked his supposed calorie burn with multiple devices. The treadmill awarded him 642 calories. The Nike system indicated 531, while the Polar heart-rate monitor's function flashed up a mere 415. For the identical activity the ActiTrainer – an accelerometer, heart sensor, and sophisticated metabolic tracking device – showed just 395. A very wide range, therefore, between about 10 calories per minute and 16 calories per minute, with the highest count some 62 per cent above the lowest count. The real count was probably closest to the ActiTrainer, which tracks body motion and heart rate, according to Dan Heil, an exercise physiology professor at Montana State University. As you add more

relevant information into the device, it has more to work with. 'It's all about processing the raw data with the best statistical methods available,' says Heil.

Calories are burned by the mechanics of moving a given mass over a certain grade at a certain speed, which is how most treadmills approach the problem. Factoring in heart rate further helps a device to estimate calorie consumption, since highly efficient runners burn fewer calories. Yet the biggest factor is the quality of a device's mathematical formulae. Electronics manufacturers are crunching more data all the time and purchasing new algorithms from scientists to sharpen their calorie counts. Adding data such as resting heart rate and VO_2 max helps to refine the calorie-counting calculations. Additional formulae based on heart-rate variability – a measure of the time intervals between heartbeats – were used in tests and predicted calorie consumption within 7 per cent of the actual amount.

Feel the Power

Moving the monitoring and evaluating of training pace and heart-rate data one stage further, wattage is now added to the mix. Cyclists and triathletes have long had this as a significant training tool, as have rowers.

'People try to draw a lot of conclusions about heart rate, but it only gives you the input, what the athlete is experiencing,' said Joe Friel in 2009, author of The Triathlete's Training Bible and part-owner of the software company TrainingPeaks. 'Power will show the true output regardless of wind, hills or surface.' Cyclists have long used power metres to measure the forces applied to the pedal by a rider's foot and judge their output in wattage. Friel says measuring the force of an athlete's shoe on the ground would be similarly useful in running – if technical challenges can be overcome. As at early 2014 there is little evidence that this has moved on. Without going into physics unduly, in cycling the wattage is readily measured by showing the cyclist's power going through the pedal, while for rowers the oar or Concept Two console is the instrument where the power is applied. For a runner the surface where the power is applied is the track or road – or a treadmill, where the belt's moving status complicates the science so that the data wouldn't be comparable to the data that a cycle or rowing test can indicate. Put simply, it seems that the measurement of running economy is, in effect, the endurance runner's proxy for wattage.

Garmin's Accuracy of Distance

This is an old bugbear and on a practical basis it has its roots in numerous runners that I have coached feeding back their Garmin-based marathon pace from some of the world's biggest and most reliably measured marathons. They are full of supposedly 26.6- and 26.7-mile routes, instead of the accurate established distance of 26.2. The likes of Berlin, London, Rotterdam and Boston marathons don't do short or long courses – they follow the IAAF (the World Athletics Federation), which demands the highest level of accuracy. It's called the Jones Method. The world's most well reputed course measurer is Hugh Jones, who won the London Marathon in 1982; curiously he isn't the Jones who invented the Method.

So, when athletes have Garmined a 26.7 mile marathon, or indeed a 10.2km route on an internationally credible 10k course, their first reaction is that they really ought to more closely follow the blue line (where there is one marked), which indicates the shortest

route available. At the back of their mind they have a slight doubt as to whether the course accuracy is all it claims to be. Only when I browbeat them about the Garmin margin of error do they bury the idea that they have somehow added half a mile of weaving off the shortest course route.

An independent 2011 survey (www.dcrainmaker.com) looked at a range of the main Garmin and rival distance measurements, covering all the market leaders. It tested them on walk, run and bike journeys across a range of accurately (Jones) measured short routes between 0.5 and 1.5 miles, and used varied course types: a straight line, a 400 metres athletic track, a typical combination route that nearly all runners will habitually use in practice, and a couple of highly wooded and underpass routes – selected because it's known that Garmin sensors are vulnerable in such situations.

The results, in summary, showed that in the wooded and underpass routes the measurements were typically 5–6 per cent short – around 25–30 seconds per mile at an 8-minute mile pace. That's a noticeable discrepancy – you'll know from experience how the perceived effort will vary significantly if you alter the pace by 30 seconds per mile. Most runners are aware of this lack of reliability in these 'difficult' scenarios. More relevant perhaps is that there was a typical 2 per cent inaccuracy in even the most simple routes. It's true that the products are marketed with a publicized 2.5 per cent margin of error, so no one's being formally misguided, but it's maybe surprising that the large majority of the products do actually have a 2 per cent level of inaccuracy.

How much does this matter? Well, if you are trotting along at a comfortable steady effort of say 9.30 minutes per mile, it maybe isn't a big deal if it's either 9 minutes 20 seconds or 9 minutes 40 seconds (that's about 2 per cent either way). If you are doing 400-metre intervals it's maybe not a worry if a 98-second split is somewhere between 96.5 and 100 seconds. But if you are trying to nail down your pace judgement at high intensity it's a discrepancy you could do without.

Where it can really hinder your enjoyment is in a race. Imagine you are chasing your first sub-45-minute 10k and you rely on your Garmin all along the route. If you are running even paced with a 2 per cent 'overscoring' Garmin, which seems to be a frequent occurrence, your watch will show you passing 9k in 40 minutes 30 seconds – supposedly smack on that 4 minutes 30 per km target you are chasing. In fact you are barely at 8.8km; you are actually running at 4 minutes 35 per km, so you have about 55 seconds additional running to complete the actual 10k distance, compared to what your Garmin is suggesting.

My advice, therefore, particularly in big prestigious races where everything is just so, is to use the actual kilometre or mile markers on the course as the most reliable indicators of how far you have run.

MENTAL SKILLS

Successful athletes have certain mental characteristics that are in many ways similar to those of people who succeed in life generally.

The mental side of sport is seen by many as a great uncharted territory which offers scope for further improvement at élite level. It's a case of 'we don't know what we don't know', which is arguably more pertinent to where we are with brain function in sports performance, compared to the progress made in understanding biology and physiology. Maybe a sports psychologist would have placed this section in the central training contents in Chapter 2 rather than in this 'supporting' section. Perhaps in twenty years' time it would be strange for a coach not to do likewise…

It's certainly true that mental qualities can be successfully applied at any level of performance. However, don't place more emphasis on the mental side than is likely to apply to your situation. Or, to be blunt, if you run twice a week at a comfortable pace and do no other aerobic training, with a VO_2 max of 46, no amount of mental skills will put in what the physiology isn't in a state to provide – you won't be able to will yourself to that 34-minute 10k.

Committed runners wish to become the best they can be within the scope of their limitations – other life commitments, finances, time, and their natural ability. They set high, realistic goals for themselves and train and play hard. They pursue their goals while enjoying their sport. Their running enriches their lives and they believe that what they get back is worth what they put in.

The Ohio Centre for Sport Psychology works with serious athletes of all ages and ability levels to help them learn and sharpen these important skills. Its research, particularly that done by Dr Jack Lesyk, identified nine specific mental skills that contribute to success in sports.

The Nine Mental Skills of Successful Athletes

1. Choose and maintain a positive attitude
2. Maintain a high level of self-motivation
3. Set high, realistic goals
4. Deal effectively with people
5. Use positive self-talk
6. Use positive mental imagery
7. Manage anxiety effectively
8. Manage emotions effectively
9. Maintain concentration

These skills are learned and can be improved through instruction and practice. The process of doing so follows the broad structure of training physical competency: an assessment of where you are currently at, a realistic goal of where you wish to get to, and an informed plan on how you will reach your goal, with periodic evaluations along the way. One main difference is that the evaluation will be more subjective – you can't empirically compare a

45-minute 10k to a 7 out of 10 for managing your emotions effectively.

Of course, across the thousands of hours that many of us have spent watching and reading about high level sports, we can all recall cases where some of the highest achievers deviate somewhat from these values. There's one great British distance runner who said that he always thought of second place as 'first loser'. One GB Olympic sprint champion – and undoubtedly one of the UK's greatest ever track athletes – said of the Olympic ethos of taking part rather than winning: 'whoever first said that must have been a loser'. Those of a certain age will recall the tennis court antics of the legendary John McEnroe being somewhat lacking in respect, managing emotions and dealing with people effectively. And let's not even start on some of the behavioural traits of Premiership footballers… However, all these successful but flawed high achievers will, for many years and usually in situations away from the public and media eye, have displayed high levels of the other qualities.

Although each of the nine skills is important, their primary importance will occur during one of three phases, which the Ohio Centre views as a performance pyramid: long-term development, immediate preparation for performance, and during performance itself. The SMART goal is included for thoroughness, while acknowledging that anyone not living in a cave will have been made aware of this acronym for some decades.

Level One: These skills provide a broad base for attaining long-term goals, learning, and sustaining regular training. They are needed on a day-by-day basis for long periods of time, often months and years.

Level Two: These skills are used immediately before performance to prepare for it, either in the general lead-in, for example 2 hours before a race, or something specific, such as thinking about your breathing pattern as you stand on the start line.

Level Three: These skills are used during the actual performance.

1. Attitude
- Choose an attitude that is predominately positive.
- View your sport to compete against yourself and learn from your successes and failures.
- Pursue excellence, and realize that you won't be perfect.
- Maintain balance and perspective between sport and the rest of life.
- Respect the sport and others in the sport.

2. Motivation
- Be aware of the rewards and benefits that you can gain through sport.
- Persist through difficult tasks, even when these rewards are not immediately achieved.
- Realize that many of the benefits come from your participation, not necessarily the outcome.

3. Goals and Commitment
- Set long-term and short-term goals that are realistic, measurable and time-based.
- Be aware of your current performance levels and develop specific plans for attaining your goals.
- Stay highly committed to these goals and to carrying out the training programme to make them happen.

4. People Skills
- Realize that you are part of a larger system that includes family, friends, maybe a coach, and others.
- Communicate your thoughts and feelings to these people and listen to them.

- Develop effective skills for dealing with conflicts, and with other people when they are negative.

5. Self-Talk

- Maintain your self-confidence during difficult times with positive yet realistic self-talk.
- Use self-talk to regulate thoughts, feelings and behaviour during competition.

6. Mental Imagery

- Prepare yourself for competition by imagining yourself performing well in it.
- Create and use mental images that are detailed and realistic.
- Use imagery during competition to prepare for action and recover from poor performances.

7. Deal Effectively with Anxiety

- Accept anxiety as part of sport.

- Realize that some degree of anxiety can help you perform well.
- Be able to reduce anxiety when it increases, without losing your focus.

8. Deal Effectively with Emotions

- Accept strong emotions such as excitement, anger and disappointment as part of sport.
- Use these emotions to improve, rather than interfere with, performance.

9. Concentration

- Know what you must pay attention to during each race.
- Learn how to maintain focus and resist distractions, whether internal or external.
- Be able to regain focus when concentration is lost.
- Be able to compete in the 'here and now', blocking out both past and likely future events.

CHAPTER 12

SO YOU WANT TO GO FURTHER?

At a coaching seminar during the Olympics hosted by one of the major shoe companies, the presenter described how in the first London marathon in 1981 some 8,000 runners completed the course in an average of about 3 hours 15 minutes. By 2012, over 35,000 people completed the course in an average of around 5 hours. Leaving aside the debate about how GB élite running has declined over this period, it does indicate that the 2012 marathoner and his or her 1981 counterpart are very different beasts, on average. The most relevant trends, which everyone in the current running world has to work with, include the following:

- Runners now tackle their first marathon with far less experience of training and competing at other distances.
- Runners now are significantly undertrained aerobically compared to the average of a generation ago.
- Runners are much less well conditioned in terms of overall physical strength and robustness than those of thirty to forty years ago. A whole host of major changes in lifestyle and school sports opportunities have contributed to this.
- On average runners compound their less robust bodies with a heavier bodyweight than your common or garden 1981 marathoner carried.

Running shoe manufacturers need to make products that serve this market. It's not in their interests to have too many of these less advanced runners – many of whom may not have hugely deep levels of long-term motivation for the sport anyway – being injured just by the running activity itself, so they have mainly focused on producing highly cushioned supportive footwear that cossets the typical runner's flawed 'structure'.

I have experience of extensive case histories because every year in about December a band of marathon newbies come to me for coaching advice for an April marathon, usually London but also, increasingly, Brighton, Paris or Edinburgh. They have been allocated a place in the ballot, have prevaricated over getting any structured long-distance training under their belt through autumn, and so the Christmas present or New Year's resolution is to 'get fit for the marathon'. Their typical longest run is in the 9- to 11-mile range; often lower leg niggles are already creeping in. They may often be quite humble in their goals, but they always want to have some sort of time goal – if it was really just about getting from A to B they wouldn't be seeking individual coaching. Typically they think that over a three- or four-month span of preparation they might reasonably aspire to repeat their current 10k pace for over quadruple the distance, and then a bit more.

My usual opening gambit, which may not win any awards in the 'anything is possible if you put your mind to it' stakes, is to defer the place for a further twelve months if they can and, at the earliest, target an autumn marathon, giving themselves a further six-month training window. If this doesn't work, I summarize why I think the timescale they are asking me to work within is definitely not in their best interests athletically, but I will do what I can. From then on it is largely a fragile balance between building up the training distance enough so that the 42.2km target becomes not unduly longer than anything they have ever done before, and not building up the distance so rapidly that they become injured in the build-up itself. In a significant minority of these cases, they don't make the start line.

This is a very general ball park figure and everyone makes their own choices about why and how they wish to train for and get through their marathons, but in the age groups up until 45 to 50 I would suggest that if you don't think running about 4 hours 40 to 4 hours 50 minutes is a realistic marathon target, defer doing the full 42.2 kilometres until this becomes feasible. Of course, many many thousands go round in slower times, but for each one of these there is maybe someone else who has not made the start line. If you are perfectly happy to complete a marathon with large bouts of walking in the later stages, that's absolutely fine, though you're unlikely to be reading this book.

Very recent medical research published in 2013 in the Canadian Journal of Cardiology has given some robust support to my views. Before anyone reads too much into the following, it is not a warning about anyone below advanced high performance level tackling a marathon, nor is it suggesting that recreational runners incur lasting damage by doing a marathon. However, the study looked at twenty 'recreational' runners aged between 18 and 60 who completed the Quebec City Marathon and had no pre-existing cardiovascular issues. A series of tests done before, directly after, and three months after the marathon showed that half of these runners had decreased left and right ventricular function three months post-marathon. The resulting effects seemed to be transient and there wasn't longer term damage, but from a coaching perspective one would not encourage runners to enter an event which could leave them with restricted cardiovascular efficiency for the following three months.

Here are some general guidelines, therefore, on where you should be at before signing along the dotted line – or maybe that should now be pressing 'Submit':

- Four months before the event you can cover at least 12 miles. The specifics about the pace aren't a worry, just that you can run or jog the whole way.
- Four months before the marathon you are running on average at least five times per 14 days. Again the exact distances per run, per week and the pace isn't such a priority, but you are in a habit and state of aerobic fitness and physical robustness whereby every 2 or 3 days you go out for a run (or even, for treadmill types, you stay in and go for a run).
- You are not in a repeated cycle of building up the running to your current level and developing an overuse injury in doing so. If this is your current status, logic suggests that the additional load to prepare you for a marathon is only going to drastically increase the likelihood of the injury(ies) recurring during the build-up.

If you are able to tick the above, go ahead.

If you have any gaps in these foundations, don't yet try to build your marathon on such shaky roots, but wait until you can cover the bases. Most people should be able to address these in a further six months, albeit the injury prevention aspect can be a frustrating and not always cheap or quick one to get to grips with.

The recreational distance running world that stops short of marathons is huge; it's diverse and it's fun. Many of the world's greatest long-distance runners have run huge mileage and had tremendous success on track, road and country without ever needing to try the marathon distance. And they never had park runs, Corporate Challenge or Race for Life on offer either.

On the assumption that readers haven't yet delved into the International Association of Athletics Federations' High Performance Coaching manuals, note that 'long-distance running' is formally categorized as 5k and beyond, based largely on how the energy systems requirements alter as one goes through the running distances. If nothing else, you need now never embarrass yourself in polite running company by saying '10k is just a sprint'.

FURTHER READING

Sports Injuries – Their Prevention and Treatment, Lars Peterson and Per Renstrom (CRC Press, 2000)

Running Fitness and Injuries, Vivian Grisogono (John Murray, 1994)

Fit to Run, Phillip Pearson (The Crowood Press, 2014)

Fuelling Fitness for Sports Performance, Samantha Stear (2004)

Food for Sport: Eat Well, Perform Better, Jane Griffin (The Crowood Press, 2001)

Complete Guide to Sports Nutrition, Anita Bean (A & C Black, 2009)

Food, Nutrition and Sports Performance II, Ron Maughan *et al.* (Routledge, 2004)

INDEX

RELATED TITLES FROM CROWOOD

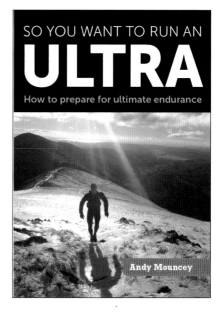